INSIGHT COMPACT GUIDE

antigua
& Barbuda

Compact Guide: Antigua & Barbuda is the ultimate quick-reference guide to this popular destination. It tells you all you need to know about the attractions of the sunkissed sister islands, from Antigua's picturesque capital, museums and bars to Barbuda's renowned bird sanctuary and powdery beaches.

This is one of 133 Compact Guides, combining the interests and enthusiasms of two of the world's best-known information providers: Insight Guides, whose innovative titles have set the standard for visual travel guides since 1970, and Discovery Channel, the world's premier source of nonfiction television programming.

Pam Barret

APA PUBLICATIONS
Part of the Langenscheidt Publishing Group

Insight Compact Guide: Antigua & Barbuda

Written by: Pam Barrett, David Howard
and Martha Watkins Gilkes
Edited by: Lesley Gordon
Photography by: Jerry Dennis
Additional photography by: Corbis 59/1, Bill Coster/NHPA 49/1
Cover picture by: Gary John Norman/Getty Images
Design: Vicky Pacey
Picture Editor: Hilary Genin
Maps: Dave Priestley

Editorial Director: Brian Bell
Managing Editor: Maria Lord

CONTACTING THE EDITORS: As every effort is made to provide accurate
information in this publication, we would appreciate it if readers would
call our attention to any errors and omissions by contacting:
Apa Publications, PO Box 7910, London SE1 1WE, England.
Fax: (44 20) 7403 0290
e-mail: insight@apaguide.demon.co.uk

Information has been obtained from sources believed to be reliable,
but its accuracy and completeness, and the opinions based thereon,
are not guaranteed.

© 2003 APA Publications GmbH & Co. Verlag KG Singapore Branch, Singapore.

First Edition 2003
Printed in Singapore by Insight Print Services (Pte) Ltd

Distributed in the UK & Ireland by:
GeoCenter International Ltd
The Viables Centre, Harrow Way, Basingstoke,
Hampshire RG22 4BJ
Tel: (44 1256) 817987, Fax: (44 1256) 817988

Distributed in the United States by:
Langenscheidt Publishers, Inc.
46–35 54th Road, Maspeth, NY 11378
Tel: (1 718) 784-0055, Fax: (1 718) 784-0640

Worldwide distribution enquiries:
APA Publications GmbH & Co. Verlag KG (Singapore Branch)
38 Joo Koon Road, Singapore 628990
Tel: (65) 6865-1600, Fax: (65) 6861-6438

www.insightguides.com

anTIGUa & BaRBUDa

Introduction

Places

Culture

Practical Information

△ **Cathedral of St John the Divine (p20)** The Cathedral contains beautiful stained-glass windows, including one depicting the crucifixion.

▷ **Redcliffe Quay (p30)** Shops and stalls jostle for space along the waterfront, one of the oldest parts of St John's.

▽ **Betty's Hope (p54)** Antigua's first sugar plantation is a valuable heritage site.

▷ **Half Moon Bay (p61)** With 365 beaches, visitors to Antigua are truly spoilt for choice, but this crescent-shaped sheltered bay is considered one of the best in the world.

▷ **The Boat House (p68)** The pillars at the water's edge are the remains of the boat and sail loft at the Dockyard.

△ **Devil's Bridge (p57)** Waves crash against the rocks and water shoots through a blowhole at this natural landmark.

▷ **Nelson's Dockyard (p67)** The Admiral's Inn in the Dockyard, which is the world's only Georgian naval facility still in use.

△ **Fig Tree Drive (p88)**
A drive through Antigua's
west coast reveals lush
tropical vegetation and
fragrant fruit trees.

▷ **Shirley Heights
(p72)** Save Sunday for a
trip to the Heights when it
is packed with visitors and
Antiguans enjoying steel
pan and reggae music.

▽ **The Lookout (p72)**
The Lookout is an ideal
place to watch the sunset
over English Harbour.

Action-packed places

Celebrated for endless strips of white and pink-sand beaches, the scattered stubs of sugar mills and a political dynasty worthy of a soap opera, Antigua and Barbuda have much to offer. Sunbathers and ornithologists have equal reason to step ashore and follow their passions. Watersports enthusiasts enjoy open access to warm waves and unrivalled underwater reefs and caverns. An added incentive to visit is that the islands are rightly perceived as safe and unthreatening.

The beaches of Antigua and Barbuda are unbeatable. A rich natural menu offers gleaming sandy bays or remote, intricate coves, largely untouched save for a rough, dusty track or visiting yacht. Offshore, coral reefs offer underwater forests of fish and other sea creatures for divers, while winds blow constantly off the east coast for the sailing crowd. The international yacht set breeze in for Antigua's annual Sailing Week every April. Leeward, western bays provide beautiful year-round bathing in clear, unruffled waters.

MORE THAN SUN, SEA AND SAND

Beyond the beach, the capital, St John's, offers a captivating glimpse of the urban Caribbean, combining the trappings of political power with the rusted-iron realities of life near the edge for the island's very poor. Warehouses have been converted into shops and restaurants, fishing boats bob alongside cruise ships in the harbour.

The wooded hills of southwest Antigua stand out in a landscape otherwise scoured for sugar plantations in the 17th century. Villages of gaily painted 'chattel houses', the husks of former mills and the ruins of Great Houses are signatures to Antigua's turbulent past of sugar and slavery. The islands of Barbuda and Redonda offer quite different vistas. The former rises barely 135ft (45m) above its coral origins. A frigate bird sanctuary draws visitors to the largest breeding grounds in the region. The latter, an uninhabited rock, once provided phosphate and guano.

Top beaches
Among the very best of Antigua's 365 beaches are: Half Moon Beach (in the east of the island), Rendevous Beach (not far from Nelson's Dockyard), Dickenson Beach (northwest coast) and Darkwood Beach (southwest coast). On Barbuda, the long sweep of Palm Beach, beside Codrington lagoon, is acclaimed for its pink sand.

Opposite and below: beach life in Antigua and Barbuda

TERRAIN

The largest of the Leeward Islands, Antigua lies on the northeast shoulder of the Caribbean archipelago, 450 miles (725km) east of Hispaniola. On frequent clear days, you can see Monserrat's volcano smoking to the southwest, while Guadeloupe's shores are visible on the southerly horizon. The state of Antigua and Barbuda includes two dependencies, Barbuda, 25 miles (40km) to the north, and the uninhabited rocklet of Redonda 24 miles (38km) to the southwest. Antigua and Barbuda were once one sedimentary land mass, scythed apart 12,000 years ago when sea levels rose and flooded the lands. Eight thousand years later, the first settlers island-hopped from the mainland and made use of the forest and cove resources.

Weaving palm-leaf hats

HISTORICAL PATHS

Developed as colonies in 1632 after the British claimed the terrain Columbus first sighted and named in 1493, Antigua and Barbuda were important points in the British imperial constellation. The Codrington family leased Barbuda as a provisions base, while the main island was deforested and devoted solely to sugar. Vast riches were made for the plantocracy, who imported slave labourers from the west coast of Africa. Over 12 million men, women and children were shipped across the Atlantic. The number of slaves on Antigua peaked at 37,500 in the 1770s, but thousands more died during the crossing.

On the same island, but worlds apart, life for the white planter classes suffered more from decadence than want. John Luffman writes in *A Brief Account of the Island of Antigua* (1789) that 'men sport several dishes at their tables, drink claret, keep mulato mistresses, and indulge in every foolish extravagance'.

The voice of the enslaved is poignantly recounted in *The History of Mary Prince, a West Indian Slave, related by herself.* This narrative bears witness to the ills of the age as experienced by a woman in

St John's during the early 18th century. Emancipation came in 1834, but not before a series of slave rebellions had ensured that the days of the regime were numbered. The most famous revolt occurred in 1736 and, if successful, would have altered the course of Caribbean history. A plot to massacre the whites of St John's was discovered at the last minute as planters and their families gathered in town for the annual ball to celebrate the coronation of George II.

Given the sugar monopoly, former slaves, once freed, had little choice of alternative work, and most remained on the plantations. For the planters, the cost of wage labour turned out to be lower than the upkeep of the slave system. With migrations of Chinese and Indian labourers during the 19th century and Dominican workers in more recent times, the Antiguan population has evolved to its present-day black majority.

COMMONWEALTH STATUS

Antigua and Barbuda was appointed an Associated State of the Commonwealth in 1967. The national flag of the sun rising on a black background with bands of blue, then white, narrowing to a 'V' for victory, bordered by red, was elaborately designed for this occasion. The sun depicts the dawn of a new era; red, symbolises the

> **Claims to fame**
> Redonda has some unusual claims to fame. Collectors battle for the rare stamps, minted by the Antiguan government as a nice little earner. And a bizarre legacy of monarchs, set in motion in 1865 by Matthew Shiell, an Irishman from Montserrat, who claimed the island as a kingdom, have bestowed literary-based titles to artists through the years. Dylan Thomas and Henry Miller were granted knighthoods, and Sting has also been given a title.

Antigua's dramatic flag

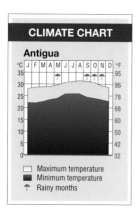

CLIMATE CHART

Antigua

☐ Maximum temperature
■ Minimum temperature
☂ Rainy months

people's dynamism; black belongs to the island's soil and African heritage; while gold, white and blue signal the soul of tourist heritage – the sun, sand and sea.

Population and Language

One third of Antigua's total population of 66,000 are concentrated in the capital, St John's, but settlements are lightly scattered throughout the island's 108 sq miles (280 sq km).

Barbuda's 1,300 residents share the main settlement of Codrington and many miles of pink sand beaches. The 1 sq mile (1.6 sq km) of rock that makes up Redonda has few visitors, except for inquisitive yachting folk. Most Antiguans and Barbudans have never been there. A marooned workforce at the end of the 19th century mined guano or phosphate, but it is now uninhabited.

The language of the islands is English, although a rich local patois, particularly among rural people, can sometimes be very difficult for outsiders to understand.

Climate and When to Go

The islands are among the driest in the region, which ensures that visitors can bask in sunny weather whenever they go. The high season

Village street after rain

between mid-December and mid-April, coincides with the sailing highlights; test match cricket attracts visitors in May and the summer Carnival draws large crowds. Hotels and airlines raise their prices during the peak season; from May to November, prices tumble, or are more susceptible to 'special deals'.

In reality, Antigua is a year-round destination, with little monthly difference in the amount of rainfall, temperature or cooling trade winds. Temperatures vary between 79°F (26°C) and 90°F (32°C), the warmest months tending to be August and September. The trade winds, a constant easterly sea breeze, are on tap to relieve the settling heat. The rainy season chiefly involves afternoon showers, euphemistically referred to as 'liquid sunshine', that come and go in a flash.

HURRICANES

The hurricane season extends from July to November. Between the 1950s and late 1980s, Antigua and Barbuda experienced only a few instances of damaging activity, but in 1989, Hurricane Hugo blew in the changes for the ensuing decade, which spawned several severe tropical storms. The most devastating was Hurricane Luís, which roared through the region in 1995. Three years later, Hurricane George wreaked havoc on the islands, while subsequent hurricanes have had nerves twitching without causing too much disruption.

Fortunately, the early warning systems and increasing awareness are helping the region to weather the storms. Modern weather forecasts and an island-wide media alert set-up provide adequate warnings several days before an approaching hurricane, so visitors can move on or be prepared. Local residents have time to shore up their property, and loss of life during hurricanes is rare if proper shelter has been sought. Airport facilities might be on hold for a few days if extreme conditions have occurred, but by and large, local flooding and the nuisance of debris are the main outcomes. If caught in a storm,

Farming

Although tropical fruit is grown on the island, there is no major crop to replace the sugar monoculture. Sweetcorn, tomatoes, and root vegetables such as sweet potatoes, dasheen and eddo are the main vegetable crops.

There is some cattle farming, but herds of sheep and goats are more commonly seen throughout the island, often wandering across the road, and devouring everything they can find. Goat is a staple food for the islanders, but given their numbers, it is surprising that it does not appear on restaurant menus more frequently than it does.

Ripening chilli peppers

however, visitors should be aware that food stocks may be limited and some hotel staff could be absent while dealing with their own property.

The environment

Given the lowest rainfall levels in the Caribbean, Antiguan and Barbudan landscapes lack the tropical lushness associated with neighbouring islands. The plantations carved away the woods and this cut in the hydrological cycle is blamed by many for the limited rainfall today. There are no rivers or streams, which heightens the value of this oft-neglected commodity. Sensitive hotels advise visitors to temper any unnecessary water usage. The higher parts of the island can offer a rainforest effect in the more richly vegetated hills of the southwest. After occasional downpours, water can rush down these hillsides, providing temporary glimpses of what might have been. Fig Tree Drive *(see page 88)* remains a celebrated route of wild bananas, lianas and would-be rainforest.

> ### National fruit
> Antigua doesn't have many commercial agricultural successes but the national fruit, the Antiguan black pineapple, stands out. The fruit, which grows in the south-west of Antigua, is unique to the island. This small pineapple, weighing about 2.2 lb (1 kg) is extra sweet and it's a delicacy that should be tried if you see it on a restaurant menu or on sale in a local market.

BIRDLIFE

Over 140 varieties of birds can be found on the islands. The yellow-breasted bananaquit, known as the sugar bird, is one of the most common and can be seen darting around brilliantly coloured blossoms. Their addiction to sugar leads them to the easy pickings of hotel and café table sugar bowls. Tiny, brightly hued hummingbirds abound, hovering amid flowering bushes. The mangrove lagoons that fringe parts of the coastline are home to herons and lumbering pelicans.

Barbuda has many species of bird, listing brown boobies, pelicans, herons, laughing gulls, terns and white-crowned pigeons. Black-necked stilts, bridle quail doves and West Indian tree ducks vie for air space with white-cheeked ducks and marbled godwits. The mangrove swamp in Codrington Lagoon is home to a nesting colony of over 4,000 frigate birds that has been closely studied and many birds tagged to provide a wealth of unequalled information.

Frigate bird in a mangrove lagoon

PROTECTING RARE SPECIES

Antigua plays host to a number of rare or endangered creatures. There are Hawksbill turtle nests on Long Island, off the northwest coast of Antigua, and the Hawksbill Sea Turtle Research Project has been undertaking crucial studies of the species since the mid-1980s. The Antigua racer snake is among the rarest in the world, with a colony of only a hundred or so inhabiting Great Bird Island. The mongoose, brought to the islands during the 18th century to control the rampant rat population that was feasting on the sugar crop, is now perceived as a pest. They may often be seen scurrying across roads into the safety of the bush. Scorpions and tarantulas, the latter locally called horse spiders, keep themselves secluded in remote dry areas.

Below: hungry bananaquit
Bottom: black pineapples

Since the 17th century, when Barbuda was leased to the Codringtons to raise livestock to feed Antigua, the descendants of the first goats and deer have roamed through the logwood and lignum vitae of the bush, surviving several centuries of human settlement. The fate of the nature reserve on Guiana Island, off Antigua's northeastern coast, has been more troublesome. The wildlife sanctuary, populated by deer and run for many years by Cyril 'Taffy' Burton and his wife, guarded the largest colony of nesting seabirds and was the sole habitat for mockingbirds in the

region. In 1997 the Burtons were forced off the island to make way for a US$300 million tourism development, but the scheme is still on ice.

Politics

The colonial schemes of the past are more than matched by today's intriguing political scene, which has thrown up corruption and money laundering matters by the bucketful. The Bird family, masterminded by the late Vere Cornwall Bird, has held stern grip on the country's political, economic and media matters for over five decades.

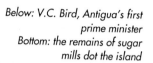

Below: V.C. Bird, Antigua's first prime minister
Bottom: the remains of sugar mills dot the island

V.C. Bird rose to power through the trade union ranks, leading the first political party, the Antigua Labour Party, to electoral victory in 1946. A brilliant orator, he wowed the masses and became the dominant political and economic force on the island. He led the Antiguan people into the postcolonial era with rousing rhetoric but made it clear in the 1950s and 1960s that the island operated as two separate societies, the whites and 'the rest'.

After the slow churning of political and constitutional cogs, Antigua and Barbuda gained independence in 1981. Queen Elizabeth II remains the Head of State for this constitutional monarchy, and is represented by a Governor General who oversees elements of the island's ceremonial pomp and circumstance.

V.C. Bird led the new state until 1994, when his son Lester B. Bird took over the reigns. As times changed, the lines of power and money became more interwoven within the Bird clan and their networks of associates. Flows of large investments from abroad, without signs of obvious gain for the people of Antigua, and an embarrassing series of offshore financial scandals, lowered the tone of government business. The late Tim Hector, editor of the opposition weekly *Outlet*, formed the Antigua Caribbean Liberation movement in the 1970s. His newspaper became a major weapon against the government and exposed the so-called 'Space Research' initiative, alleged to be a front for arms laundering.

A critical insight into the island's social structure and politics is given by Antiguan-born author Jamaica Kincaid in her widely-acclaimed book, *A Small Place* (1988).

> **Home from home**
> Times have changed little since Kenneth Pringle wrote dismissively of the union between cruise ship tourism and Caribbean culture in *Waters of the West* (1939): 'They travel in boats which are floating replicas of the more expensive quarters of the towns they have left, complete with cinema shows, snack bars, balalaikas, and radios, and while on the first stage of their peanut pilgrimages do everything in their power to forget they are on the sea.'

TOURISM AND THE ECONOMY

Sugar was a cruel king for much of Antigua's economic past. Christopher Codrington could survey his lands and pronounce that, 'Everyone that is able is working upon sugar, which is certaine gaine.' As world prices waned in the mid-18th century, its dominance lessened and the economy began to falter. Revived to an extent by US military investment during the 1940s and 1950s, infrastructure was put into place to develop a new economic presence, that of upmarket tourism. At the time, many Barbudans saw migration as the only prosperous route and it still is perceived as important for income-earning potential.

Tourism has dramatically changed both islands, as international air travel has increased. Today, around two-thirds of the working population are employed in a tourist industry which provides 60 percent of the national income. The benefits have largely outweighed the costs; new forms of more sensitive tourism have been pioneered, and the range of activities and events in which tourists may engage has been extended to the benefit of islanders and visitors alike.

Fish is now less important to the economy than tourism

HISTORICAL HIGHLIGHTS

BC 2400 Nomadic Siboney or 'stone people' populate the island, now known as Antigua.

AD 35 The Arawak or 'Wadadli' pastoral groups establish agricultural and trade systems.

1100 The Caribs conquer Arawak lands and install supremacy over the Leeward Islands.

1493 On his second voyage to the Americas, Columbus sights the island and names it Santa María de la Antigua.

1525 Spanish settlers land on the island, but are soon forced to withdraw due to illness and resistance from the Caribs.

1632 After sporadic attempts by French and Spanish missions to claim the island, it is colonised by a British expedition from St Kitts, under Sir Thomas Warner. First settlement established at Parham.

1640 The Carib chief kidnaps the Governor's wife and takes her to Dominica. In revenge, Warner's son invites the Caribs to a feast at which they are all slaughtered.

1666 St John's is briefly held by French forces, who destroy the town.

1674 Christopher Codrington establishes the first sugar estate at Betty's Hope, which remains in the family for almost 200 years.

1680 The neighbouring island of Barbuda is leased to the Codrington family, who raise livestock and agricultural products with slave labour for the British colonists on Antigua.

1736 A plot to kill all whites in St John's during the annual ball is discovered at the eleventh hour. Fear and rumour spread of further slave insurrections.

1748 Sugar is actively produced on the island by 170 mills and plantations, laying the foundations of the colonists' vast wealth.

1784 Horatio Nelson arrives as captain of HMS *Boreas*, based in English Harbour. Antigua's importance for the British navy as a regional command post increases throughout the 18th century.

1807 The slave trade is abolished by Britain, although slavery itself persists on the plantations.

1830s–40s Antigua is hit by earthquakes, hurricanes, drought and yellow fever, and a fire destroys most of St John's.

1834 Slavery finally abolished. Some 29,000 slaves are freed, without the four-year changeover period of 'apprenticeship' imposed on other islands.

1842 The island's first cricket club is founded by the 59th Foot Regiment of the British Army on New Year's Day.

1850s The sugar industry is thrown further into crisis by reduced commodity prices, hurricanes and drought. In just over a century, Antiguan sugar production ends.

1865 Matthew Shiell, an Irishman from Montserrat, claims the rock, Redonda, for his son Philippe. The kingdom is passed to the poet John Gawsworth, who declares himself King Juan I, distributing titled largesse to the literati.

1938 The Moyne Commission for the West Indies records Antigua as among the most impoverished of the islands.

1939 In response to miserable working conditions, the Antigua Trades and Labour Union is formed and comes under the leadership of Vere Cornwall Bird, a former Salvation Army officer and soon-to-be premier.

1941 Anglo-American destroyers-for-bases deal extends US influence in the region and creates a US facility at Coolidge Air Field, today the V.C. Bird International Airport.

1946 The first local elections are won by the Antigua Labour Party, an offshoot of the union, led by V. C. Bird.

1961 The restored Nelson's Dockyard is reopened as a working port and a tourist attraction.

1967 Antigua, with Barbuda and Redonda as dependencies, become an Associated State of the Commonwealth. The first Antigua Sailing Week is held at English Harbour and continues as an annual event.

1968 The deepwater harbour in St John's opens, enabling Antigua to become a popular port of call for large cruise ships.

1971 The last sugar plantation on Antigua ceases production. The so-called 'Broom Election' sweeps the Progressive Labour Movement and George Walter to victory, clearing out the Bird administration. Five years later, however, a 95 percent turnout returns V. C. Bird as premier. The Birds, the late V.C. and now his son, Lester, have remained in power ever since.

1981 'Papa' Bird leads Antigua and Barbuda to independence on 1 November. The first test match is held in Antigua, during which a local player, the 'Master Blaster', Viv Richards, knocks off a century.

1986 On home turf, Viv Richards scores the fastest century in world cricket against England.

1988 Jamaica Kincaid's *A Small Place* is published and damned by many for her sharp criticism of Antiguan society. The book is still not for sale on the island.

1989 Always resistant to Antiguan interference, the Barbuda People's Movement gains all nine seats on the Barbuda Council and campaigns vociferously for greater autonomy. The Antiguan government and Bird family come under scrutiny during allegations of arms and finance dealings with South Africa and Israel. A British Commission accuses the government of 'unbridled corruption'.

1992 Three opposition parties merge to form the United Progressive Party in an attempt to overthrow the Bird dynasty and the Antigua Labour Party.

1993 V.C. Bird retires from political life aged 84 years, and his son assumes leadership of the Antigua Labour Party. Lester B. Bird becomes Prime Minister the following year.

1995 Hurricane Luís causes chaos and US$300-million of damage.

1997 A series of financial scandals and the collapse of a major Antiguan bank under suspicious circumstances provoke international condemnation of the island's financial sector.

1999 Lester B. Bird is re-elected as Prime Minister.

2002 Tourism, which has grown rapidly over the past three decades, increases its monopoly of the economy, employing a third of the working population and generating about 60 percent of the island's income.

Map on page 21

1: St John's

St John's was founded by English colonisers around 1660, and although it was invaded and occupied by the French a few years later, it soon reverted to English control. Over the next 200 years sugar made it prosperous, but it went downhill in the mid-19th century after the emancipation of slaves, a reduced demand for cane sugar and a radical drop in prices.

It is an easy little city to find your way around on foot, as it is laid out on a grid system. If you are driving, you must remember that many of the streets are one-way, but there is no real need for a car. There is a small car park to the left of Market Street, and another at Heritage Quay.

Covering some 4 sq miles (10 sq km), St John's has a population of about 31,000, roughly half that of the whole island. Although some of the modern developments are undistinguished, there are plenty of attractive 19th-century buildings, some rather dilapidated, but many of them well renovated after damage by hurricanes, earthquakes, fires and years of neglect.

Unless you are coming straight off a cruise ship, the best starting point for a walking tour of the city is the Cathedral of St John the Divine.

Below: colonial buildings
Bottom: St John's Cathedral

CATHEDRAL OF ST JOHN THE DIVINE

The skyline of St John's, the island capital, is dominated by the 70-ft (21-m) twin towers of the ★★ **Anglican Cathedral Church of St John the Divine** ❶ (open during daylight hours). The great parish church, with its walled, shady churchyard, covers a wide block between Newgate and Long streets. The towers, topped with shiny grey cupolas, are impressive, especially for those arriving by sea (which about half of the island's visitors do), and have earned St John's the reputation of 'the most imposing of all the Cathedrals in the West Indies'.

It is also called 'a church within a church', because after the first, wooden structure built on this site in 1683–84 was destroyed by fire, and a second, stone building severely damaged by the great earthquake in 1834, it was decided that radical measures were needed. Consequently, the present building, completed in 1847 and consecrated on 25 July the following year, was given a pitch pine interior and a stone exterior, as a defence against both fire and earthquake. Subsequent minor tremors and the earthquake of 1974 have taken their toll, however. A great deal of renovation was completed in time for the 150th anniversary in 1998, but work is still going on.

The iron gates on the south face of the church, in Long Street, are flanked by pillars displaying lead figures of St John the Divine and St John the Baptist. They were taken by HMS *Temple* in 1756, from a French ship destined for neighbouring Martinique, during the Seven Years' War between England and France. The cathedral can be entered through these gates, through those on Newgate Street, or via small gates on either side.

Star Attraction
● **The Cathedral**

Saints guard the gate

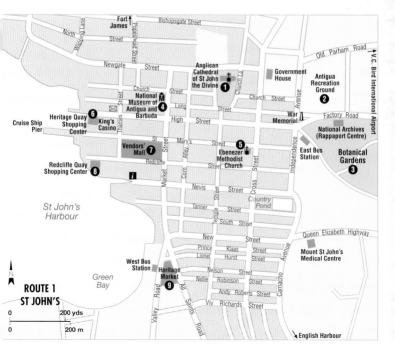

ROUTE 1
ST JOHN'S

Map on page 21

The Interior

The cruciform interior of the church includes an octagonal high altar, made of mahogany, which was presented in 1926 in memory of Robert McDonald, a former chancellor of the diocese. The beautiful stained-glass windows that allow light to flood over the altar portray the Crucifixion of the Lord with the Virgin Mary and St John the Divine.

The Blessed Sacrament Chapel is located to the left of the high altar and the War Memorial Chapel is on the right. An informative historical pamphlet is available in the church (leave a small donation to assist the seemingly endless need for restoration funds). If you are interested, there is also information about the church's history at the nearby National Museum of Antigua and Barbuda *(see page 25)*.

The first service of the day is held at 6am (except Wednesday, when it is at noon) and there are several other services on Sunday.

Below: stained-glass in the cathedral
Bottom: Government House

Government House

Nearby, east of the cathedral on Independence Avenue, is **Government House** the office of the Governor General, the British Crown's representative on the island. Originally called Parsonage House, due to its proximity to the cathedral, it was owned by a wealthy local man, Thomas Nasbury Kerby. When a suitable official residence was sought for the new governor, Lord Lavington, in 1800, the house was rented by the government because it was 'detached and pretty'. The following year it was acquired as a permanent home for the island's governors and additions were made to enlarge and embellish it. The house was extended again in 1860 in preparation for a royal visit by Prince Alfred, who was travelling on HMS *St George*.

Government House fell into disrepair over the years, until major renovations were begun in 1996. When they are completed, part of the house will be open to visitors (for more information, tel: 462 0003, or contact the Tourist Office).

THE CENOTAPH

The **Cenotaph** stands at the top of High Street, which runs into Independence Avenue. It is a monument to the Antiguans who died in World War I, and was unveiled in August 1919, almost a year after the war ended. Special services are held here each Remembrance Day (the Sunday nearest 11 November) to honour those who lost their lives during both the 20th-century world wars. A fence was placed around the monument by the Royal Air Force Association in 1965.

ANTIGUA RECREATION GROUND

The ★ **Antigua Recreation Ground** ❷ is on busy Independence Avenue, with Factory Road running along its south side. This is the site of the main national and international sporting events held on the island. It is one of the finest cricket pitches in the Caribbean and Test cricket is played here between February and May. On match days the ground comes alive and the streets outside are lined with stalls catering to the crowds, with everything from grilled lobster and spare ribs to whole coconuts, soft drinks and beer.

The exuberant annual Carnival celebrations, which last for 10 days in July and August (marking emancipation on 1 August 1834), are centred on the Recreation Ground, too. The ground is also

> **Information on the Rec**
> For more information on events taking place at the Recreation Ground contact the Antigua and Barbuda Tourist Board, tel: 462 0029/0125 (corner of Friendly Alley and Nevis Street) or the Sports Manager, tel: 562 1682.

A quiet moment at Antigua Recreation Ground

Map on page 21

Below: Gravy dances at all the test matches
Bottom: refreshment stall opens for business at the Rec

used for big parades, including the Independence Day Parade on 1 November, celebrating Antigua's independence, and the Queen's Birthday Parade, held early in June. Football is played here, too, and the Montserrat national team trained here after their own ground was destroyed as a result of the volcanic eruption in 1995.

The government-owned ground, known locally simply as 'the Rec', can seat 9,000 spectators in covered stands and can accommodate up to 15,000 standing – and often does. There is no admission fee unless an event is being held.

NATIONAL ARCHIVES

Opposite the Recreation Ground, on the other side of Factory Road, is an angular white building, the **Rappaport Centre**, which houses the **National Archives** (Mon–Thur 8.30am–4.30pm, Fri 8.30am–3pm). The archive stores a wealth of information about the island, which used to be kept in the National Museum before the completion of this purpose-built centre.

BOTANICAL GARDENS

The centre stands in landscaped grounds that border the **Botanical Gardens** ❸, spread over 8 acres (3 hectares), with vehicle access running

around their perimeter. The gardens were established in 1893, with the aim of providing a green and open space in the bustling capital and promoting an awareness of the natural environment.

At one time they were a popular spot but in the 1960s they deteriorated and for some time they were rarely used. Some restoration work was carried out in 1987 by the Botanical Gardens Society, but the society itself declined over the years, and two major hurricanes took their toll on the grounds during the 1990s.

Plans are about to be finalised and funding should shortly be approved to enable the Ministry of Agriculture to get to work on the gardens and restore them to their former glory.

Star Attraction
● **National Museum**

WORTHY SPECIMENS

However, the gardens are a shady spot in which to cool off in the middle of a hot day's sightseeing or shopping, and there are still some plants worthy of note. There is a majestic old tree called the zulu tree *(Ficus nekbuda)* which is nearly 90 years old. There are also specimens of Cuban royal palm *(Roystonia regia)* and the so-called sausage tree *(Kigelia africana)*, as well as bamboo *(Bambusa vulgaris schr.)* The lignum vitae tree *(Guiacum officinale 1.)* can also be found here. It is known locally as 'iron wood' because it is extremely hard and was therefore used in many of the sugar mills, the remains of which still dot the island.

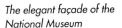

The elegant façade of the National Museum

NATIONAL MUSEUM

Going back (west) down Long Street, past the Cathedral of St John the Divine, to the corner of Market Street, you will reach the ★★ **National Museum of Antigua and Barbuda** ❹ (Mon–Fri 8.30am–4pm, Sat 10am–2pm; US$2 donation suggested; tel: 462 1469). The stone building, which was originally St John's Old Court House, was constructed in 1747 on the site of the first city market, and is the oldest building still in use in the city. It was designed by an English-born architect, Peter Harrison, and financed by a tax

Map on page 21

levied on local slave owners. The court of justice was held on the ground floor of the building and the upper floor was used as the Council and Assembly meeting room.

Telling the Island's Story

The Historical and Archaeological Society of Antigua and Barbuda operates the museum, which it established in 1985. The ground floor houses an interesting selection of exhibitions which tell the story of the island, from its geological birth to political independence in 1981.

There is a fine collection of Amerindian (mostly Arawak) artefacts, brought from various sites all over the island, and displays on sugar production, including a steam engine, and on the mid-19th century emancipation of slaves.

Also on display is the cricket bat that belonged to Viv Richards. In 1986 he used the revered bat to score the fastest test match century in history. Viv Richards, one of the most famous and popular West Indian cricketers of all time, is a local hero. He has a street named after him in St John's and a statue of him is planned, to share space with that of ex-prime minister V.C. Bird in Heroes' Park (*see page 32*) next to Heritage Market.

On the upper floor is a meeting hall where programmes of lectures are held. Also on this floor is the Patterson Memorial Gallery, an educational space that focuses on the environment and its protection. The Historical and Archaeological Society organises monthly field trips and cultural evenings and there's an interesting little gift shop on site.

Conservation concerns

The Environmental Awareness Group (EAG) office is located on the top floor of the National Museum building. Set up in 1989, it aims to raise awareness about the importance of the island's natural resources and the need for conservation. The group does a great deal of educational work throughout the island, and is part of an international project with a mission to save the rare racer snake (*see page 48*) and to protect other indigenous species (tel: 462 6236).

Viv Richards' bat in the National Museum

Ebenezer Methodist Church

From the Rec you could have chosen instead to walk down High Street, where busy vendors' stalls crowd the first stretch of pavements, or the parallel St Mary's Street, both of which lead to the quays. The latter would take you to **Ebenezer Methodist Church** ❺, constructed in 1839. Methodist teaching on the island was inspired by a prosperous plantation owner, Nathaniel Gilbert, who was a Speaker in the House of Assembly. Inspired by the preaching of John Wesley (1703–91) in England, he brought the message home to Antigua. The first chapel was built here in 1786, but so popular was Methodism that the congregation quickly outgrew the small building and a larger structure was needed. Unfortunately, the subsequent one was badly damaged in an earthquake in 1843 and again in 1974. On both occasions it was repaired, then in 1982 it was declared a historical landmark and work was carried out to strengthen the structure.

Below: Ebenezer Church
Bottom: old and new buildings side by side in St John's

Historical though it may be, the exterior is not architecturally very interesting, and the building is usually only open when services are in progress (Sunday at 8am). It is sometimes used as a concert venue, however, and if you pop in when one is in full swing or being set up, you will find a pleasing, airy interior with a wide wooden gallery running around three sides.

THE HIGH STREET TO THE QUAY

Walk west down High Street now, where the most imposing buildings belong to banks. Barclays is pink-washed, the Bank of Canada is colonial in style, and two solid, pillared edifices house the Bank of Antigua. At the end of the street, on the

Map on page 21

right, is the rear of the post office, beside which stands a small bronze statue of Vere Bird, known as 'Papa Bird', the first prime minister (and father of Lester Bird, the present one) and the most dominant figure in the island's history.

THE CASINO

Approaching from this direction, **King's Casino** (daily 10am–2am; tel: 462 1727; www.kingscasino.com), will be your first introduction to Heritage Quay. The casino opened in 1988 and, although it is not the only one in Antigua, it is the largest. Gambling choices include roulette, Caribbean poker, craps, baccarat, black jack and state-of-the-art video-poker as well as a wide selection of slot machines. In this air-conditioned haven there is also an opportunity to gamble online. Players are provided with free drinks. There are two ATM machines that accept all major credit and debit cards, and a spacious sports bar with a 10-ft (3-m) television screen which shows major sporting events.

HERITAGE QUAY

The casino was built to cater to the needs of passengers from the cruise ships that call at the modern, 900-ft (274-m) dock that was constructed in St John's Harbour in 1988. During the high

Moravian memorial

At the end of High Street, in front of the casino, is the Westerby Memorial Fountain. It commemorates George Wall Westerby, Bishop of Moravia, who died in 1888 after 'labouring faithfully in the West Indies for nearly 50 years', as the inscription reads.

The Moravian sect began in Bohemia in the 15th century, resurfaced in Moravia in the 18th century, then spread to the Americas, reaching Antigua in 1765. The mission was to take the gospel to all oppressed people and provide both primary and secondary education for slaves.

There are 15 Moravian churches on Antigua, all well attended by the devout islanders.

A cruise ship docks at Heritage Quay

season (November to April), three or four huge ships from the major cruise lines dock here each day, disgorging passengers for a day on the island. The dock is being further extended to cope with demand during these months, although out of season when there may be only four or five ships a week, it looks a little forlorn.

★ **Heritage Quay ❻**, the adjoining duty-free shopping complex (Mon–Sat 9am–6pm, and Sun and public holidays when cruise ships are in dock) grew up at the same time. Here you can buy high-quality jewellery at Columbian Emeralds and Diamond International, Cuban cigars at La Casa del Habano, spirits at Quin Farara's Liquor Store, Prada and Gucci bags, belts and wallets, expensive perfumes, photographic supplies, and some very down-market souvenir mugs and ashtrays. There are public lavatories in the complex and facilities for disabled travellers, including access ramps. When ships are in port, there is sometimes live steel band music, too.

Quin Farara's liquor store has a choice of spirits

THE VENDORS' MALL

Next door to the dock, encompassing a whole block between St Mary's and Redcliffe streets, is the purpose-built, ochre-coloured ★ **Vendors' Mall ❼**. On the ground floor, open to the street, are stalls run by local vendors, selling craftwork, colourful sarongs, beads and bracelets and a variety of T-shirts. Before the modern mall was built in 2001, as an extension of the Heritage Quay complex, stall holders occupied little wooden shacks, which blocked access to nearby streets. Some of the lively hustle and bustle of a West Indian market has been retained in this more organised setting.

On the upper floors of the four-storey building a luxury hotel is due to open. It is anticipated that its downtown location will make it a popular choice for well-heeled business travellers who want to be close to the centre and its attractions. A rooftop restaurant, which will have stunning views over the town and the cruise ship harbour, is also planned.

Map
on page
21

Communications centre
A good place for Fedex services as well as phone, fax, e-mail and internet facilities is Parcel Plus, boldly painted in red, white and blue, on the street side of Redcliffe Quay.

Stalls and shop fronts at Redcliffe Quay

REDCLIFFE QUAY

The south side of the vendors' mall opens onto Redcliffe Street, along the other side of which runs ★★ **Redcliffe Quay** ❽ (opening hours as for Heritage Quay), spread out over the waterfront area. This is one of the oldest parts of St John's and in 1991 was awarded a prestigious preservation award, recognising it as an outstanding example of the rehabilitation of authentic West Indian Georgian architecture.

This used to be at the very heart of the flourishing coffee, rum, sugar and slave trade between Europe, Africa and the island, and it now has marina docking for yachts from all over the world. It's an attractive development, with the well-restored, 17th- and 18th-century dockside warehouses converted into shops, restaurants and cafés, enhanced by vivid climbing plants and shady palms trees, and it has the atmosphere of a small island village.

SHOPPING AND EATING

You can buy hand-made jewellery from the Goldsmitty and designer clothing by Ralph Lauren, Calvin Klein, Guess and Sean John, as well as Mexican pottery and Indonesian furnishings, cool linen clothes from A Thousand Flowers, and beads and bags from RastaPasta. Restaurants and cafés offer a wide range of international food, vegetarian dishes and Caribbean specialities, and there are also pasta and pizza houses and good coffee and pastries *(see page 110)*.

One restaurant worth visiting for its decor and its good, island-style food is the Redcliffe Inn, a converted warehouse in which machinery from old pumping stations has been skilfully integrated into the cool and shady interior. You can also sit on covered patios at the back and front, and watch the world go by.

The Pirates' Lair bar sits on the end of a jetty, and when the *Jolly Roger* – a red-sailed galleon that offers 'pirate adventure cruises' around the coast – is in port, it adds spice to the 18th-century, buccaneering theme of the quay.

HERITAGE MARKET

From Redcliffe Street, turn right on Market Street and walk to the fork where the road divides into Valley and All Saints roads. Here, opposite the West Bus Station, you will find the ★★ **Heritage Market** ❾ (daily until 6pm). This vibrant vegetable and fruit market used to be held in the street, but is now housed in a high-ceilinged, purpose-built structure. Although it is open every day, it is best visited on Friday or Saturday morning when it is at its loudest and busiest.

Colourful, fragrant tropical fruits and vegetables are in abundance here; look out for juicy mangoes, papaya, pineapples, star fruit, custard apples, sweet little bananas (locally called figs) and guava. You may also see dasheen, breadfruit and plantain filling the wooden stalls (*see page 109* for descriptions of these fruits and some of their uses). Often the market stocks a mixture of locally grown food and produce imported from nearby Dominica and other islands where tropical fruit is more easily grown because there is higher rainfall. There are also stalls selling bright tropical flowers – ginger lilies and anthriums, again imported from Dominica.

Next door, in a smaller but otherwise identical building, is the Craft Market, selling locally made souvenirs, such as banana leaf hats, rag dolls, beads and carvings.

Star Attractions
● Redcliffe Quay
● Heritage Market

Below: enticing customers aboard the Jolly Roger
Bottom: local art for sale in the market

Map
on page
21

OUTSIDE THE MARKET

Leaving the fruit and vegetable market by the side exit you will face a small, landscaped space called **Heroes' Park**. Looming large here is an imposing statue of Vere Bird. As already mentioned, it will be joined by a statue of the cricketer Viv Richards.

Over the road, beside the ever-busy bus station, is the open-air fish market and even if you don't want to purchase fresh fish it is worth wandering through to see the wide variety of glistening fish and exotic-looking seafood on sale. Next door is the meat market – not recommended for the fainthearted. The whole area is very lively on Friday and Saturday evenings.

ST JOHN'S MEDICAL CENTRE

Heading east from here along Viv Richards Street from the market brings you to Camacho Avenue, a continuation of Independence Avenue. Turn left, and on a small hill at the intersection with Queen Elizabeth Highway, you will see a modern building, **Mount St John's Medical Centre**. This US$50 million facility was completed in 2003 as Antigua's main public hospital, replacing the nearby Holbertson Hospital. A welcome benefit for patients is one of the most spectacular views on the entire island.

Scottish settlers
Market Street used to be known as Scots Row because of the number of Scottish traders who settled there in the 18th century, and made a living dealing in textiles and other goods.

Fish fresh from the sea in the fish market

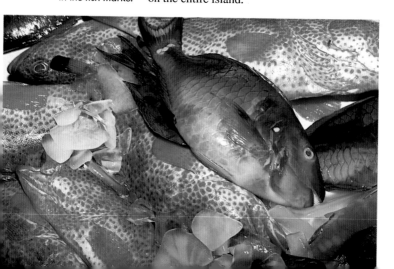

2: The North Coast

Map on pages 50–51

Fort James – Runaway Bay – Dickenson Bay – Jumby Bay – Fitches Creek – Parham – Crabs Peninsula – offshore islands

Leave St John's via Popeshead Street, which becomes Fort Road, and follow it round the north side of St John's Harbour. Apart from the fort and two excellent beaches this coast does not have a great deal to offer visitors, but there are some interesting corners and byways. The off-shore islands belong geographically in this route, but can usually only be visited on boat or catamaran trips that pick up visitors from St John's or from hotels all over the island *(see page 117)*.

Star Attraction
● **Fort James**

CLOSEST BEACH TO TOWN

The road curves round towards **Fort Bay**, passing Millers By The Sea, a great seaside restaurant and café, which also does take-aways *(see page 110)* and follows the sweep of **Fort James Beach**. This is a pleasant white sand strip that is very popular with local families at weekends and on public holidays, as it is the closest good beach to town. There are lots of refreshment, barbecue and souvenir stalls, in season, and loud music at weekends. A swimming club trains here, too (the safest and best swimming area is marked) and in the early morning there are regulars who have been coming here for years.

Fort James Beach is the closest to St John's

FORT JAMES

From the beach, paths have been laid out among the trees, leading to the remains of ★★ **Fort James** (always open), which is approachable on foot or by car. On a site originally called St John's Point, the fort was built, along with Fort Barrington *(see page 80)*, to protect the entrance to the harbour from enemy ships and pirate incursions. The foundations were laid in the 1670s, a few years after the French had sacked St John's, but the the walls did not go up until early in the 18th century. When it was completed it had 17 cannon,

Map
on pages
50–51

which were increased to 36 during the American War of Independence (1775–83) at the time that Britain got very edgy about the islands. The fort never engaged in battle but it must have been a successful deterrent.

Ten of the huge cannon remain, as do some the original walls. Fort James is next in line for National Park status, and when funds become available, major restoration work should begin. At present, apart from the magnificent view, it is the size and the site that are most impressive, and the battery of great guns facing out to sea – a sight that would have been enough to deter any approaching ship.

RUNAWAY BAY

Back on the main road, turn left and, passing a lushly-landscaped health centre and the Island Inn, a guesthouse that would not look out of place on the coast of Devon, take another left turn to ★ **Runaway Bay**. Some of it was washed away in the storms caused by Hurricane Luís in 1995, but this long beach is still attractive, although not as pristine as some of the others on Antigua. There is a wide choice of restaurants and beach bars along here, including the Casino Riviera, a restaurant as well as a gaming house, that is the favourite choice of many local people at Sunday lunchtime,

Masons' stone
A plaque on the wall of Fort James states that the first stone was laid by William Isaac Matthew, the Provincial Grand Master of the Three Lodges of the Free and Accepted Masons of Antigua.

Cannon still guard the ruined Fort James

and Lashings, which promises pizzas till 2am *(see page 110 for restaurant details)*. Several planned time-share condominium developments may mean that Runaway Bay will soon become busier.

McKinnon's Salt Pond, bordered by mangroves and a certain amount of rubbish, parallels the road and the beach, and is a good place for birdwatching – sandpipers, terns, pelicans and herons are at home here.

SWIMMING WITH DOLPHINS

Across from the salt pond is ★★ **Dolphin Fantaseas** (tel: 562 7946, fax: 562 3646 or e-mail: antigua@dolphinfantaseas.com to arrange bookings). This swimming-with-dolphins enterprise opened, amid great controversy, in 2001. A lagoon has been created in a dredged mangrove swamp, containing 5.5 million gallons (25 million litres) of water, in which live three dolphins – two males who interact with staff and visitors, and a female who prefers to keep herself to herself. Visitors, who are provided with the appropriate gear and given a brief educational talk, are taken into the lagoon in small groups. There they can stroke, feed and swim with these mammals, as well as with the stingrays in a separate pool.

It is the kind of enterprise that tends to divide people firmly into two camps – those who are appalled that dolphins should be kept in captivity at all, and those who relish the opportunity to get close to them and learn more about them, and are prepared to pay a hefty sum (US$105 per person) to do so.

CORBISON POINT

The coast road to Dickenson Bay takes you via Corbison Point, which divides the two bays. Set high on a neat green bluff is a conical stone structure that at first sight could be a renovated sugar mill, but is in fact the remains of an 18th-century British fort. Fragments of Amerindian pottery have been found on this site, but no traces of any early civilisation are visible.

Star Attraction
● Dolphin Fantaseas

Below: lashings of fun at Lashings
Bottom: a local beachcomber

Map
on pages
50–51

DICKENSON BAY

Running between Corbison Point and Weatherills Point, the mile-long sweep of ★★ **Dickenson Bay** beach is almost unbelievably white, its waters stunningly turquoise-blue. Windsurfers and waterskiers love it, but there is also a protected swimming area so that they don't encroach on those who prefer to laze or swim.

This is one of the most heavily populated tourist areas on the island, so it can get busy at the height of the season. The two main hotel-resorts here are the couples-only **Sandals**, and the **Rex Halcyon Cove** *(see page 124)*.

The main road now goes inland; a left turn just after Weatherills Farm leads back towards the coast. The **Blue Waters Beach Resort** *(see page 123)*, at Soldier Point, is well known as a venue for weddings, as are Sandals and many other hotel-resorts on the island *(see page 121)*. The latticed wedding gazebo can be seen on the clifftop.

Taste of home
On Wednesday and Friday between 4.30 and 9pm, an English family serves fish and chips from a van on the road outside Buccaneer Cove at Dickenson Bay, just past the Siboney driveway. It's inexpensive, very busy and popular with ex-pats.

Sandals Resort for a romantic holiday

DETOUR FOR GOLFERS

Follow the road now via Boon Point to the residential district of Crosbies, then turn right on Friars' Hill Road (which leads back into St John's). You will pass a tropical nursery, Oasis Plants, and the remains of two sugar mills, Langford's and Dunbar's. On the left is the 18-hole Cedar Valley

Golf Club, one of two golf courses on the island that are open to the public *(see page 114)*.

MODERN MALLS AND A SUGAR MILL

As you drive down Friars' Hill Road the so-called **Sleeping Indian** can be seen in the distance. A small range of hills – Leonard's Hill and Saddle Hill – make up what appears to be the silhouette of a recumbent Indian figure.

Jasmine Court, a modern mini-mall complex, is on the left of the road. It includes Paradise Gym, which has every type of exercise machine imaginable. Visitors are welcome to take out short-term membership, or even hire the services of a personal trainer, some of whom are trained in the USA. There is also a fragrant flower shop and a pleasant open-air restaurant in the complex.

About half a mile (1km) from Jasmine Court, Woods Centre is a bigger shopping mall with the largest supermarket on the island, The Epicurean, a modern, American-style shop, with everything one could wish for. Next door, Woods Pharmacy is well-stocked and the staff are helpful. There is also a bank, a dry cleaners, a photo shop, a post office and a variety of other services.

Going back up Friars' Hill and turning right towards the coast, you will reach the affluent residential area of **Hodges Bay**. This is the site of the oldest occupied house on the island (not open to the public). It can be seen to the right of the road, just before the remains of a sugar mill. Parts of the house date from the 17th century and it has a magnificent open kitchen hearth, which was used until 1916. The estate's slave burial ground is on the south side of the road.

ISLAND ARTS GALLERY

The ★★**Island Arts Gallery** (Mon–Sat 9am–5pm) is on a narrow road leading from Alton Place, near the Hodges Bay Hotel (it is signposted). The owners, Nick and Gloria Maley, originally from the UK, have created a delightful spot, with flowering gardens and a large selection of exotic

Star Attractions
● Dickenson Bay
● Island Arts Gallery

Below: Rex Halcyon Cove
Bottom: golf at Cedar Valley

Map on pages 50–51

tropical birds. As well as being a painter, Maley was a Hollywood special effects make-up artist who worked on films such as *Star Wars*.

There is a wide variety of inexpensive tropical prints, locally-made, hand-crafted artefacts and Nick's vibrant paintings and sketches, as well as works by Antiguan and other Caribbean artists. From time to time there are exhibitions of works by international artists. Island Arts has a special display showing the history of Maley's work in film, including rare *Star Wars* prints and other unusual movie memorabilia. When visiting the gallery ring the bell even if the wrought iron gate is locked, or better still, telephone before setting off (tel: 461 6324).

Other outlets
The products of both Island Arts and The Pottery can also be founded in St John's, the former in Heritage Quay Shopping Centre, the latter in Redcliffe Quay.

Work in progress at Island Arts

JABBAWOCK BEACH

Follow the road around the coast to Beggars' Point and ★ **Jabbawock Beach**. Originally named for a nightclub which ceased to exist years ago, it is a totally natural spot, that is popular with local people. The Antigua and Barbuda Defence Force, which has 'adopted' it, looks after its maintenance and keeps it beautifully clean.

From the point and the beach you can see **Prickly Pear Island** off-shore, a very popular destination for day trips. Miguel's Holiday Adventure has been operating charters to the island for 25 years. After a five-minute trip, guests reach the secluded island where a lobster lunch is included in the price.

CAMP BLIZZARD

Follow the road, and after a short while take a sharp left. This brings you to a crossroads and, on the left, is the Antigua Defence Force's **Camp Blizzard**, housed in what was the US Naval Base (still shown as such on maps). The US leased the land from 1941 until the early 1990s when they handed it back to the Antiguan government. Turning left, you will reach the end of the road after a few hundred yards. On the right of the gated entrance to the military camp there is an unpaved road which leads to ★**The Pottery** (Mon–Fri 8.30am–3.30pm; tel: 461 0369 or 562 1264). Sarah Fuller makes and sells individually designed pottery using local clay and Caribbean blue glazes.

The terracotta clay is dug in the central plains of the island, air dried and stored until it is needed. Many of the designs reflect the island's colourful history and indigenous features – sugar mills, pineapples and exotic blooms, for example. Beyond, The Pottery there is nothing but a scruffy little beach, where pelicans swoop down to snatch fish from the water.

Below: Antigua Air Station
Bottom: a pot takes shape at The Pottery

TRACKING THE ROCKETS

Go back to the crossroads and turn left; this will take you along the bottom of the airport runway. En route you pass the Antigua Air Station, its sign mounted behind cannons and two ancient coppers that were boiling vats from an old sugar mill. This station is a vital part of the US Air Force Space Command's global network of missile and satellite tracking stations. It is over the skies of Antigua that satellites launched from Cape Canaveral in Florida go into the earth's orbit. The radar and telemetry systems here track the rockets during this critical manoeuvre and instantaneously send the data back to the Cape for analysis.

Map on pages 50–51

JUMBY BAY

Along this airport-skirting road (with Winthorpes Bay to your left) you will reach the **Antigua Beachcomber Hotel**. The Jumby Bay ferry dock is located here and is the only access to the luxurious **Jumby Bay Resort** on **Long Island** *(see below)*. Day passes are available for people who are not staying at the hotel. These entitle them to make the 10-minute ferry crossing in the morning and return in the late afternoon. Passes include lunch, tea, use of non-motorised watersports facilities and access to the swimming pool (for details contact Jumby Bay on tel: 462 6000).

St George's Church overlooks Fitches Creek Bay

TURTLE PROJECT

Jumby Bay is home to one of the greatest natural wonders on Antigua, the Hawksbill Turtle. Among the most endangered species of sea turtles, the Atlantic Hawksbill *(Eretmochelys imbricata)*, has always been prized for its beautiful shell and the jewellery that is produced from it. In 1987 the ★★★ **Jumby Bay Hawksbill Turtle Project** was born, as people became aware of the valuable nesting ground here. This project is funded by the Jumby Bay Club and by private donations, along with assistance from the Institute of Ecology at the University of Georgia, which organises and co-ordinates the project.

According to the Wider Caribbean Sea Turtle Recovery Team and Conservation Network (WIDECAST), this nesting site is one of the most important and best studied rookeries of hawksbill turtles in the entire Caribbean region.

CONTRIBUTING TO THE PROJECT

Guests at Jumby Bay Resort can join the all-night vigils, assisting in research activities by documenting turtle activities, as well as observing. In the off season, and by special arrangement during the season, Antiguans and visitors not staying at the resort can also join in (contact the Environmental Awareness Group, tel: 462 6236; or John Fuller, Box 1168, St John's, tel: 462 0485).

Mid-June to late November is the most active laying season; contrary to popular belief, turtles lay not once but several times a year. In an average season 25–30 turtles nest here at Pasture Bay.

Star Attractions
● **Jumby Bay Hawksbill Turtle Project**

FITCHES CREEK

Follow the road that parallels the runway, and turn off to the left to find **St George's Church**, in a splendid setting overlooking Fitches Creek Bay. An Anglican church built in 1687 and remodelled some 50 years later, it was badly damaged by Hurricane Luís in 1995 but has been restored and now has a new roof. In the large graveyard surrounding the church is the tomb of an early English settler, William Barnes, who died in 1695.

Dawn's Nursery, which has been operating since 1987, is down a left turn past the church. Hibiscus, bougainvillaea, orchids and a wide selection of colourful tropical plants are on sale here, including indigenous species such as calabash, the silk cotton tree and passion fruit.

Fitches Creek is an up-and-coming residential area on the bay. Spreading out from the traditional village street are roads dotted with smart villas, their gardens full of flowering trees and palms. New roads are being laid out and there are a number of signs announcing that building plots and development land are for sale.

Below: at Dawn's Nursery
Bottom: one of the modern villas at Fitches Creek

Map
on pages
50–51

BUMPY ROUTE

For the adventurous, and those with four-wheel drive vehicles, there is a route on back roads that runs along the seashore from Fitches Creek to Parham. This route has been used as an illegal dumping site for some years, and although serious efforts are being made to clean it up, it is now the most scenic route to travel, although there are birds to be seen in the mangrove swamps that border the bay.

TRACKING THE SATELLITES

A better, if longer, route is to follow the straight road that parallels the airport runway. It passes the 80-ft (24-m) American satellite tracking antenna, part of the Antigua Air Station. With this large antenna and a smaller one just below it, operators capture the data that reveal the position, systems status and health of the missiles and satellites hurtling around the earth's orbit at 17,500 miles (28,000km) an hour. This information is instantaneously transmitted to analysts in the USA who use it to assess the performance of the missiles and improve future ones.

The two smaller antennae are the command/destruct aerials, which send coded signals to destroy a missile that has gone astray and could endanger a land mass. Once destroyed, the missile

The Pitch

On the waterfront, just past the island's satellite tracking antenna is The Pitch (daily 10am–10pm; tel: 461 1417), a bar/restaurant that screens worldwide sporting events. It is a popular local eating spot, with local specialities like pepperpot stew (containing salt beef, pumpkin and okra), seasoned rice, Creole fish, seafood water (a stew containing all types of seafood), cockles and curried beef.

Taking it easy

nd its payload falls harmlessly to earth. The site s not open to the public.

The road makes a slight left turn then joins the main Factory Road, where you turn left, and go past the Antigua Sugar Factory *(see page 52)* until you reach a left turn with a big outdoor barbecue stall on the corner. This is the road to Parham.

Star Attraction
● **St Peter's Church**

PARHAM HILL ESTATE

Travelling towards Parham, the mill towers of **Parham Hill Estate** (private, not open to visitors) can be seen on the right, as can the tall, graceful Royal Palms surrounding the house. Royal Palms were once associated with all the colonial Great Houses on the Caribbean islands, usually lining the driveways. Parham Hill is one of Antigua's finest remaining examples of these houses. Built in 1689 for the wealthy Tudway family (who at one time also owned Guiana Island), it stayed in the family until the late 19th century. Surrounding the house are the ruins of disused sugar factory buildings, including a windmill, the smokestack of a steam-driven sugar-grinding machine that came into use during the 19th century, and various sugar processing buildings. There are also outbuildings that housed the staff and served as guest rooms. The house has been lovingly restored and repaired after damage by several recent hurricanes.

Octagonal St Peter's Church

ST PETER'S CHURCH

The little town of **Parham**, located at the end of the road, features one prominent building, ★★ **St Peter's Anglican Church** – take a left turn, where ochre urns stand on tall plinths at either side of the track. This was the first building in the village to be lit by electricity, in 1920. The present church is the third to be built on this site; the first, constructed in 1711, was a wooden structure that burned down, leaving only a walled graveyard in the open countryside. Interesting gravestones from some of the old island families remain in the overgrown churchyard. The second church, built

Map on pages 50–51

in 1754, was dismantled to make way for the present one, built in 1840. This light, airy building is octagonal in shape and features a beautiful ribbed, ship's keel ceiling and some of the original stucco work. It is one of the finest examples of Georgian colonial architecture in the Caribbean. The roof was damaged during Hurricane Hugo in 1989 and underwent major repairs in time for the 150th anniversary of its dedication, on 29 June 1990.

Below: a typical village house
Bottom: sleepy Parham Harbour

PARHAM VILLAGE AND HARBOUR

There are some pretty wooden houses and refreshment stalls in the village of Parham, but there is not much more. It was the first British settlement on the island and the home of one of the early British governors. Because of this, some people claim that it was the original capital, but this is not the case.

Parham's sheltered port, the first on the island, flourished with the sugar trade, but today it only offers anchorage for a few pleasure yachts and a small fleet of fishing boats. It is sometimes possible to hire a boat to take you out to the offshore islands. To the left of the harbour an area is being developed for the use of local fisherman and as a market place for tourist-oriented goods, which should bring some revenue to the little village.

ANTIGUA BREWERY

Turn left as you leave Parham to reach the low, flat stretch of Crabs Peninsula, which comes to an abrupt end at the Antigua Defence Force military installation. Just before this, on the right of the palm-fringed road, is the **Antigua Brewery** (Tues–Fri 8am–3pm for guided tours of approximately an hour; tel: 463 8115/7515 or call in). The brewery produces three beers, including Wadadli, the famous flagship brew (named after the aboriginal name for Antigua), a pale lager pioneered in 1993 that has won awards. Guinness, Coca-Cola and numerous other soft drinks are also produced here, including a popular local tropical fruit drink. The German-owned brewery sponsors a number of island events, including Antigua Sailing Week, the Balloonfest, the Oktoberfest and Carnival.

NORTH SOUND ISLANDS

From the east of Crabs Peninsula, it is easy to see the islands that lie in North Sound. The largest is Guiana Island, separated from the mainland by The Narrows, a strip of water about 400ft (120m) across. The offshore islands also include Great Bird, Little Bird, Lobster, Hell's Gate, Red Head, Rabbit and Exchange islands. They are all uninhabited and can be reached by boat. Small private charters can be arranged, but most people see them from boat or catamaran trips around Antigua's coast *(see page 117 for details).*

A VARIETY OF WILDLIFE

The North Sound islands offer a rare opportunity to appreciate the glories of nature, both above and beneath the water. As you glide along in a boat you can look down and see small stingrays below. Some of the endangered species found in these islands include the West Indian whistling duck *(Dendrocygna arborea)*, the tropical mocking bird *(Mimus gilvus)*, the Antiguan ground lizard *(Ameiva griswoldi)* the red-billed tropic bird *(Phaethon aetherus)* and the hawksbill turtle

> ### Desalination
> Also located on Crabs Peninsula is the Antigua Distillery and the Water Desalination Plant, built in 1987. Although visitors will not get too excited about this, it is worth remembering that on an island that suffers from severe water shortages, it is desalination plants that enable hotels to provide you with warm showers and flushing toilets.
>
> Some desalinated water is used for agriculture, too, but it is an expensive process and one that is not yet widespread.

Enjoy a local brew

Map on pages 50–51

(Eretmochelys imbricate), as well as numerous other nesting birds and other varieties of wildlife.

Obviously, visitors to the islands must be aware that the wildlife should not be disturbed in any way; this is especially true for nesting birds and their young, once hatched.

GUIANA ISLAND

★★ **Guiana Island** (352 acres/142 hectares) is believed to have been first occupied as early as 2,000BC by Amerindians, but it was named after the English settlers who came here from Guiana (now Surinam) when it was taken over by the Dutch after the Treaty of Breda in 1667 and they were forced to leave. Sugar cane, cotton and staple provisions were grown by the English settlers in the early years, and the island was later taken over by Charles Tudway of Parham Hill. In 1812, it passed into the hands of Sir William Codrington, a member of one of Antigua's oldest landowning families, and it remained in the family until 1929.

Under the later ownership of Guiana Island Farms, a Welsh couple, Taffy and Bunnie Bufton, were brought to Antigua to manage the land, on which the main crop was cotton. When this was deemed unprofitable, the island was allowed to revert to nature and the Buftons remained as caretakers, looking after a herd of merino sheep, whistling ducks (now an endangered species on Antigua) and a herd of fallow deer. There were at least 100 deer in the herd, some so tame they would eat from the Buftons hands.

Introduced species
Fallow deer, were introduced to Guiana Island by the Codringtons in the 1730s to provide meat for their plantation workers. Their likeness can be found on the Antiguan coat of arms.

Boats for hire

UNIQUE SANCTUARY

According to an expert from the Smithsonian Institute, 'Guiana Island is of outstanding interest and is worthy of preservation.' The report went on, 'The Buftons created a sanctuary on Guiana that is unique in the Antilles.' Despite this, plans for a hotel development were proposed and the Buftons forced to leave. Mr Bufton died soon afterwards, but his wife is still living in accommodation provided by the government.

Sadly, many of the deer disappeared. A few volunteers have assisted with the remaining members of the herd, transporting water to the island during periods of drought. Occasionally fresh deer tracks indicate that some are still living there, but no one knows how many. The hotel development never took place and Guiana has again been left to go wild. It is home to guinea-fowl, wild ducks and an abundance of bird life. There has been talk of another hotel development but no plans have been confirmed.

There are a few scattered remnants of Amerindian sites on the island, shards of pottery and other artefacts, but these are on protected sites and must not not be disturbed. Guiana Island also has several beautiful beaches and at weekends and public holidays a few boats can be seen moored here, and local people picnicking on the sands.

GREAT BIRD ISLAND

★★★ **Great Bird Island** (25 acres/10 hectares) lies to the north; it is the next largest and the most popular for local people and visitors on day-trips to picnic and swim. Around 20,000 visitors come here annually. There are two beautiful white beaches, on opposite sides of the island, and patches of coral reefs surrounding it that make it a (careful) snorkeller's paradise.

Star Attractions
● Guiana Island
● Great Bird Island

Below and bottom: picnic on Great Bird Island while local inhabitants look on

Map
on pages
50–51

Great Bird is home to the red-billed tropic birds, which nest on the cliffs on the eastern side of the island between December and June and are seen taking advantage of the wind currents as they fly in search of fish. They are easily identified by their flowing tail streamers which are about half the length of the adult's body. Sometimes, however, their tail feathers are plucked off by aggressive frigate birds, which you will also see overhead. They are so lazy that they attack the tropic birds and steal the fish they are carrying, rather than diving to catch their own.

Failed plan

Rats have always been a problem on the islands. Centuries ago, plantation owners introduced the mongoose to kill off rats that were attacking the sugar cane. Unfortunately, the plan did not work and the island now has a surplus of mongooses, which are also regarded as pests. You will often see the long, low creatures (rather like ferrets) scuttling across the roads.

RARE RACER SNAKE

Great Bird also hosts what is believed to be the world's rarest snake. The Antiguan racer *(Alsophis antiguae)* is completely harmless and is being conserved by the Antiguan Racer Conservation Project (ARCP), a collaborative effort with six local and international partners, whose mission is to conserve threatened coastal and marine species as well as this critically endangered reptile. When the project began in 1995, only 50 snakes were found. In 2001, the census revealed 102 snakes, so efforts are paying off.

A major factor was removing rats from the island, which not only caused the racers to double in number but also increased the population

Coral arch on tiny Exchange Island

of tropic birds and whistling ducks, many of whose eggs had been devoured by the rodents.

The grey-blue females are slightly larger than the silvery-tan males, reaching just over 3ft (1m). The snakes are active in the early morning and late afternoon and often keep out of sight during the heat of the day. They feed on three lizard species found on Great Bird. One new racer colony has been established on a nearby island under controlled conditions and plans are underway to locate the snakes on other sites in the hope of increasing the population.

Below: red-billed tropic bird
Bottom: pelican on the water

HELL'S GATE

Tiny **Hell's Gate Island** is especially interesting as there is a spectacular 20-ft (6-m) coral archway, formed by erosion. Just under the arch is a small pool with a sandy beach forming a natural swimming pool. It is said the island gained its name because the waters are only a few feet deep on one side of the arch, but plunge to great depths on the other side – almost down to hell, in fact. A number of rare birds nest on this island, including the brown noddy tern *(Anous stolidus)* and Zenaida doves *(Zenaida aurita)*.

A WONDERFUL BIRD IS THE PELICAN

Rabbit Island is known not for its rabbits, but for a large resident population of nesting brown pelicans *(Pelecanus occidentalis)* living on the western side. There probably isn't a bird that gives more pleasure to the observer than the pelican as it glides soundlessly down to catch a fish. Once a fish has been spotted the bird makes a spectacular plunge into the water, with wings tucked in.

From a protective distance on a boat off Rabbit Island, the pelicans can be seen tending their nests, feeding their young and pecking at neighbours. Pelicans nest in colonies and the nest space is determined by the distance that the bird can stretch towards it neighbour. Two to four eggs are laid at a time and both parents share the task of sitting on them till they hatch.

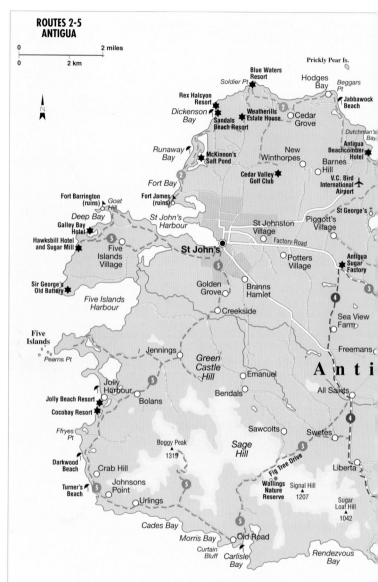

ROUTES 2-5
ANTIGUA

0   2 miles
0   2 km

N

Prickly Pear Is.

Blue Waters Resort
Soldier Pt
Hodges Bay
Beggars Pt

Rex Halcyon Resort
Jabbawock Beach

Dickenson Bay
Weatherills Estate House
Cedar Grove

Sandals Beach Resort
Dutchman's Bay

Runaway Bay
McKinnon's Salt Pond
New Winthorpes
Antigua Beachcomber Hotel

Fort Bay
Cedar Valley Golf Club
Barnes Hill

Fort Barrington (ruins)
Goat Hill
Fort James (ruins)
V.C. Bird International Airport

Deep Bay
Galley Bay Hotel
St John's Harbour
St Johnston Village
Piggott's Village
St George's

Hawksbill Hotel and Sugar Mill
Five Islands Village
St John's
Factory Road

Sir George's Old Battery
Five Islands Harbour
Golden Grove
Branns Hamlet
Potters Village
Antigua Sugar Factory

Five Islands
Pearns Pt
Creekside
Sea View Farm

Jennings
Green Castle Hill
Freemans

Jolly Harbour
Emanuel
A n t i

Jolly Beach Resort
Bolans
Bendals
All Saints

Cocobay Resort

Ffryes Pt
Sawcolts
Swetes

Darkwood Beach
Crab Hill
Boggy Peak 1319
Sage Hill
Liberta

Turner's Beach
Johnsons Point
Fig Tree Drive
Wallings Nature Reserve
Signal Hill 1207
Sugar Loaf Hill 1042

Urlings
Cades Bay
Morris Bay
Old Road
Rendezvous Bay

Curtain Bluff
Carlisle Bay

C A R I B B E A N   S E A

ATLANTIC

OCEAN

LEEWARD ISLANDS

Sombrero ◦

Dog Island ◦

Anguilla

St Martin

0   100 miles

0   100 km

St Barthélémy

Saba ◦

Sint Eustatius ◦

Barbuda

St Christopher
(St Kitts)

Nevis

Antigua

Redonda ◦

Montserrat

Leeward Islands

◦ Aves

Guadeloupe

Les Saintes ◦◦

Marie-
Galante

*Jumby
Bay* ★ Jumby Bay
Resort

**Long
Island**

*Winthorpes
Bay*

**Maiden
Island**

North Sound

**Great Bird
Island**

◦ **Hells
Gate
Is.**

*Witches Creek
Bay*

*Crab
Peninsula*

**Rabbit
Is.** ◦

**Guiana
Island**

*Parham
Harbour*

○ **Parham**

♂ **St Peter's**

*Guiana
Bay*

**Crump
Island**

**Pelican
Island**

*Mercers
Creek
Bay* ◦

Long Bay

Indian Town Pt

★ **Devil's Bridge**

★ **Cedar Hill
Estate House**

Seatons ○

Glanvilles ○

Willikies

*Nonsuch
Bay*

**Green
Island**

g u a

○ **Pares**

★ **Betty's Hope**

*Potworks
Dam*

○ **Newfield**

B R O W N S ★ **Harmony
Hall**

◦ **York Is.**

○ **Freetown**

Bethesda ○

○ **St Philips**
♂ **St Philips**

★ Half Moon
Beach

*Half Moon
Bay*

Soldier Pt

Monk's Hill
★ **Great George
Fort (ruins)**

○ **Falmouth**

★ **Calamaran Club
Marina**

**English Harbour
Town**

*Falmouth
Harbour*

⚓ **Clarence
House**

**Dow Hill
Interpretation
Center**

★ **St James
Club**

Mamora Bay

*Willoughby
Bay*

★ **Nelson's
Dockyard**

♦ **Shirley
Heights**

**Galleon
Beach**

*Indian
Creek*

Map on pages 50–51

3: East of the Island

Betty's Hope – Seatons – Devil's Bridge – St Philip's – Harmony Hall – Half Moon Bay

The southeast of Antigua is the least developed part of the island. Most of the coastline lies along the rough, exposed Atlantic with breezes blowing directly from Africa. There are few hotels but numerous beautiful beaches, many of them quite isolated, some lovely, uninhabited islands, a coastline fringed by mangroves and one of Antigua's most interesting historical sites.

This route will include some of the island's most intriguing sights, from the restored sugar mill at Betty's Hope via Devil's Bridge blowhole to the deserted beach at Half Moon Bay.

Below: mangroves near Seatons
Bottom: east coast boating

LEAVING TOWN

Leave St John's via Queen Elizabeth Highway. The new white and yellow buildings you pass on the left are government offices and a court house; the largest, standing above the others, surrounded by a high chain link fence, is the prime minister's office. To the right of the road is the Ministry of Exterior Affairs.

MEMORIALS AND MILLS

A short way along, near the intersection with Airport Road and Factory Road, there is a large expanse of fenced-off land on the right, and a sign proclaiming that it is the National Memorial Park. The area is due to be developed as a memorial to Sir Vere Cornwall Bird, former prime minister of Antigua, whose residence, and final resting place, is adjacent to the land.

The abandoned **Antigua Sugar Mill** on the left of the road can easily be identified by the tall chimney and several ruined buildings still standing. The Antigua Transport Board is also on the left; this is where temporary driving licences can be issued for visitors, but most people get them from the hire company when they rent a car.

SIGHTS ALONG THE ROADSIDE

On the right the massive red and white antennas mounted on seven 250-ft (76-m) masts are part of a short-wave relay station that broadcasts the BBC World Service and the German World Service to North, South and Central America. This is a joint venture between the BBC and the Voice of Germany under the Caribbean Relay Company, which was started in 1976. The masts carry 18 antennas and have survived unscathed all the hurricanes that have hit Antigua in recent years. Special tours and information are available for the technically minded (tel: 462 0436).

A little further along on the right is a large, well-kept farm with a variety of rare breeds. Arabian and Appaloosa horses (white with dark spots) are bred here, along with Shetland ponies. There is also a herd of white, hump-backed Zebu cattle, a breed brought here from St Kitts and Nevis that can survive drought conditions. Mr Winter, the owner of the farm, will give tours of the farm to passing visitors as and when his schedule allows, and it can make an interesting excursion.

Historical details
If you are interested in the history of the island and its earlier residents, go to the National Museum in St John's and ask for Desmond Nicholson's book, *Heritage Landmarks*. It may also be on sale in The Map Shop, St Mary's Street, St John's, tel: 462 3993; and in the gift shop at Nelson's Dockyard.

CEDAR HILL ESTATE

Off to the left, with the remains of a sugar mill barely visible, **Cedar Hill Estate** is now a private residence and is not open to visitors. Records

Isolated beach at Indian Town Point

Map
on pages
50–51

show that the landowners in the mid-18th century were the Byam family and that in 1842 it belonged to William Byam who was the vicar of Kew.

Cedar Hill is unlike the other plantation houses around the island in that the construction is of brick, as well as the more usual stone and timber. It seems that brick was used here simply because it is not far from Parham Harbour, where ships dumped the ballast of bricks that had been used to stabilise them during the Atlantic crossing. Apparently the builders of Cedar Hill decided to incorporate the abandoned bricks in the construction of the house when it was begun in 1688.

BETTY'S HOPE

Continuing along the main road (past the turning taken on Route 2 for Parham), you will reach the village of Pares. Along the roadside here, and in many other parts of the island, you may see sweetcorn being roasted over a coal fire at open-air stalls. This is an Antiguan speciality and has a crunchy, nutty texture, well worth trying.

Just outside Pares a signposted track on the right leads to ★★★ **Betty's Hope** (Tues–Sat 10am–4pm; tel: 462 4930; US$2 donation is requested). This was Antigua's pioneer sugar plantation; established in the 1650s by Governor Christopher Keynall, it became one of the most

*Below: a cheerful young Antiguan
Bottom: windmills at Betty's Hope*

prosperous plantations and flourished, thanks to slave labour, for over 250 years. The estate was taken over by the Codrington family, who already had other plantations on Barbados. Christopher Codrington was Governor General of the Leeward Islands from 1700 to 1704, and the family owned nine other plantations in Antigua during the 18th century. With the decline of the sugar trade the estate was allowed to fall into complete disrepair and many of the stones in the Great House were removed for use in local buildings. However, in 1990, the value of this site was realised, and a conservation project was initiated.

Star Attraction
● Betty's Hope

RESCUING THE PAST

Part of the former estate has been allocated as a heritage site, and a museum and visitor centre has been developed in an old stable block. One unique feature of Betty's Hope is that it had twin windmills, one of which has been well restored, complete with sails, using some machinery and artefacts gathered from other ruined mills on the island. On special occasions it can be seen in operation but even when not working it is still an impressive sight.

Perhaps more impressive – certainly more moving – is the brief, illustrated history of slavery described in the museum. This is one of the best places in Antigua to gain an insight into the sugar industry that made the island landowners so wealthy, and the slave trade that made it possible.

Recognition
Betty's Hope was recognised by UNESCO and awarded a grant in 1994. It received the 1996 Ecotourism Award for preserving the island's cultural, agricultural and industrial heritage.

Island flora

SEATONS

Return to the main road and turn right, and after about 1 mile (2km) take a left turn to **Seatons**, a pretty village that straggles downhill towards the sea. It used to be a much bigger place but in the 1950s, after a severe hurricane, many villagers moved to **Glanvilles**, a short distance east along the main road, where there was land available, and founded a new village. Seatons used to live by fishing, but many of the fishermen now work in the tourist industry.

Map
on pages
50–51

SEA MOSS

There are two interesting attractions in Seatons.
One is the ★★ **Antigua Sea Moss Project**. Sea
moss is the Caribbean name for a type of edible
seaweed that elsewhere is known as carrageen.
It is said to be beneficial for many conditions
including thyroid complaints, ulcers, congestion
and bronchitis. It has a very high nutritional value
and is reputed to boost energy levels, which may
be why it is also considered to be an aphrodisiac.
The seaweed is dried, washed and boiled until it
reaches a gluey consistency; spices are added and
it is sold as a drink. You will see SOCA sea moss
advertised outside shops and garages around the
island. It's nicer than it sounds.

Below: examining sea moss
Bottom: a kayak made for two

Trips by small boat to the sea moss farm in a
sheltered bay (you can get out and swim in the
6-ft/2-m water if you want), can be organised
through the Seaton Village Marine Management
Unit (tel: 463 2520). Ring in advance, or pop into
the Sea View Supermarket and ask for Aldrick
Nicholas, who is based next door.

KAYAK ECO TRIP

The second attraction in Seatons is the ocean
kayak trip run by ★★ **Antigua Paddles** (tel: 463
1944, fax: 463 3344) – you'll see their signs along
the road as you approach the village. This is a
well-run operation that takes small groups of visitors on a motor launch through Mercer's Creek
to the near offshore islands. There they propel
their kayaks between the tiny islands, stopping
every so often for a talk on the ecology of the mangrove vegetation that surrounds them.

When thoroughly exhausted, the party gets
back on the launch and are taken to Great Bird
Island *(see page 47)* for a short hike to the top,
then they are kitted out with snorkels for a spot of
exploration around the coral reef, or a swim from
the tiny beach, if they prefer. After that, it's back
to base for rum punch and banana bread on the
patio. It's a safe and friendly set-up that allows
you to learn quite a bit about the wildlife and eco-
logical concerns of the area.

DEVIL'S BRIDGE

Back on the main road, you pass through Glanvilles and Willikies en route to Devil's Bridge (about 3 miles/5km from the Seaton turning). Just before Devil's Bridge, on the right, there is a small bay called Hog's Hole, where there's a magnificent little white sand beach, an ideal secluded picnic spot. There is also a protected coral reef here that is ideal for snorkelling.

★★**Devil's Bridge** is a remote, wild site at the end of a narrow promontory. The area is known as Indian Town Point, although no archaeological remains have ever been found here that showed evidence of Indian settlement. The 'bridge' is a remarkable example of wind and salt-water erosion. It is a natural arch, approximately 30ft (10m) long by 7ft (2m) high, carved in the limestone rocks by the waves rolling in from Africa, some 3,000 miles (5,000km) away. There is a blowhole that produces an impressive spout of sea water, rather like that of a whale. The waters surrounding it are always rough, pounding against the coast, and the rougher they are, the more impressive the spout.

Some say Devil's Bridge gained its name because desperate enslaved Africans from nearby estates would commit suicide by throwing themselves from it into the sea, so local people would say, 'the devil have to be there'.

Star Attractions
● Sea Moss Project
● Antigua Paddles
● Devil's Bridge

Mispronunciation
The odd name 'Willikies' came about through a simple mispronunciation. Like many villages on the island it was named after the major local landowner, and this one was called Wilkins. The name was accepted, entered on maps, and has remained ever since.

Water spout at Devil's Bridge

Map
on pages
50–51

HEADING EAST

Retrace your route now almost as far as Betty's Hope and look out for a road on the left that is signposted to Harmony Hall *(see page 60)*. After about 1½ miles (2km) you come to a T-junction where a petrol station is perched on top of a small hillock. A right turn would take you to Potworks Dam, but we are going left, then first right, towards St Philip's.

After a short way you will pass Lyons Estate, on the right, which is now a private residence; it is marked by a splendid agave plant outside the grounds *(see box)*. Just past the house, on the left, is Lyons Bakery, which bakes delicious fresh bread; if you are there in the early morning you can get it straight from the oven. A few yards further along on the right is the Road House Café, a good place to stop for local food or just a cold drink.

The century tree

The tall agave karatto is Antigua's national plant. It is also called the century tree, because some of them live for 100 years – although they are not actually trees. However, once their brilliant yellow flowers have withered, the plants die. They have a use, even then: their dried stalks are strapped together and made into rafts, called Daggerlogs. The rafts used to serve utilitarian purposes, and today Daggerlog racing is a popular pastime.

ST PHILIP'S CHURCH

There isn't much to the village of St Philip's, but ★ **St Philip's Church** is worth a stop. The first parish church was built here in 1690, then rebuilt in 1830. Hurricane Luís took the roof off this one in 1995, but it has been replaced with green roofing. Judging by its smart new red roof, the house next door probably suffered a similar fate.

St Philip's is a pleasing, stone-built structure,

Dressed up for a wedding at St Philip's Church

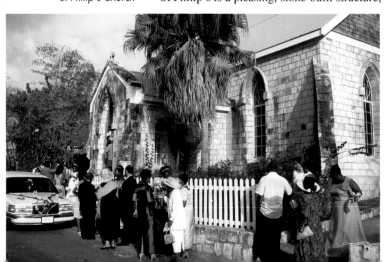

with tall windows allowing lots of light inside. It is not usually open, except for services at 6.30am and 10am on Sunday, but the churchyard is a peaceful spot, and the view over Willoughby Bay is not only beautiful, but atmospheric. Even on a calm day it is easy to imagine hurricane force winds whipping across the water, threatening the exposed buildings on the clifftop.

REGENERATION AND RUIN

Just past the church, by a small pond in a field on the right, is more evidence of the dangerous power of Hurricane Luís, and the regenerative powers of nature. The 100-ft (30-m) Hurricane Tree refused to give up when it was felled by the winds in 1995. Sprouting fresh green shoots it is still growing in a horizontal position.

The ruins of Montpelier Sugar Factory, reputed to have been one of the finest in the Caribbean in the 1890s, lies on the outskirts of the village, although there is not much to be seen from the road. Much of the equipment remains, but while there is talk of restoring the factory and opening it to visitors there are no firm plans or funding.

FLAMBOYANT TREES

As you pass the ruins and round a sharp corner four large Poinciana *(Demonic regia)*, usually known as flamboyant or flame trees, form a canopy over the road. In June and July, when they are in full bloom, covered with dazzling, bright red flowers, they are an unforgettable sight. There are stories of visitors travelling to Antigua just to see these trees in their full glory. The tree, a native of Madagascar, is umbrella shaped and offers generous shade. It blooms profusely then loses its leaves during the dry season, appearing almost dead, but as soon as the rains come new growth begins. The seed pods are long (up to 2ft/50cm) and when dry make a distinctive rattle. They are popular as percussion instruments, locally called shack shacks (rattlers). You may see varnished versions of them for sale in souvenir shops.

Below: agaves grow all over the island
Bottom: flowers of the flame tree

Map
on pages
50–51

FREETOWN

Breathtaking views of Willoughby Bay continue as you follow the main road – a good, well-surfaced one for some distance. A narrow viewing point has been created on the roadside to allow photo opportunities and encourage drivers to keep their eyes on the road as they travel. This is the way to Half Moon Bay.

Less than 2 miles (3km) from St Philip's you come to a left turn, signposted to Harmony Hall. This takes you through the lively, well-cared-for village of **Freetown**. As its name suggests, this was one of the first free villages established on the island after emancipation in 1834 (Freemans and Liberta are two of the others).

Continue straight through the village until you are offered a choice of two tracks, one going straight ahead, the other turning right. Take the former, which runs through wooded terrain past scattered ruins of sugar mills, and leads to Harmony Hall – although the signs have petered out by now. At the far end of the track (about 1½ miles/2km), when you have crossed this eastern peninsula and arrived in the district of Browns, a sign reappears, instructing you to turn right.

★★ **Harmony Hall** is an art gallery and restaurant and has accommodation in half a dozen chalet-style buildings *(see page 124)*. The sister establishment to Harmony Hall in Jamaica, it has been open since 1987. The whole place closes from mid-May to late October, but in season there are monthly art exhibitions with work by a variety of local and international artists. It is serious about promoting indigenous art and crafts and has become the centre of the island arts community.

Harmony Hall also has one of the best restaurants on the island, featuring Italian cuisine with a Caribbean flair. A sugar mill has been renovated and turned into a bar, with a circular staircase winding around it, from which there is a spectacular view, overlooking Nonsuch Bay and the nearby islands. Steps lead down through landscaped gardens to a tiny white beach, where a boat and a few ocean kayaks wait for hotel guests who want to put to sea.

Pictured in their prime
The sugar mills whose remains can be seen along the track to Harmony Hall were part of Archibalds and Colebrooks factories. There are pictures of them, when fully functioning in the 18th century, in the museum at Betty's Hope.

View over the bay from Harmony Hall's windmill bar

HALF MOON BAY

Returning to the main road, turn left, and in a couple of miles you will come to one of the most beautiful beaches on the island – although there are lots of contenders for that title. The great crescent of ★★★ **Half Moon Bay Beach** was voted by the US Travel Channel as among the top 10 beaches in the world. At one end there are rolling waves, wonderful for surfing and windsurfing; at the other, a coral reef shelters a calm bay, perfect for swimming and sunbathing.

The Half Moon Bay Hotel, wind-battered and worse for wear, has been closed since Hurricane Luís tore holes in its fabric in 1995. There are no other buildings or commercial enterprises here and the beach is totally natural. On the path down to the sand you will pass Smiling Harry's Beach Bar. Harry, who comes from Freetown, serves modestly priced local foods, soft drinks and beer.

WALK TO SOLDIER POINT

For the fit and adventurous, there's a walk, starting just beyond the hotel, that will take you along the beach and over the sharp-edged cliffs to Soldier Point, where there is a natural coral bridge poised high above the crashing waves. The scenery is spectacular, and you are unlikely to meet anyone else along the way.

Star Attractions
● **Harmony Hall**
● **Half Moon Bay Beach**

Below: jetty at Harmony Hall
Bottom: Half Moon Bay

MILL REEF

If you had continued on the main road east when you rejoined it after the Freetown turning, instead of taking the road to Half Moon Bay, you would have come to the gate of the **Mill Reef Club**, a private and prestigious organisation that has been here since 1949. With luxurious homes, a hotel where guests can only stay at the invitation of Mill Reef members, a yacht basin and marina and a golf course, this is a club for the seriously rich. The original members were mostly Americans, but now also include a number of wealthy people from other countries.

The club is one of the largest employers on the island – at least during the months when guests are in residence – and its members have been generous with sponsorship of local causes over the years.

DRY FOREST

One of the advantages of such an exclusive area as Mill Reef, is that it has allowed dry forest to flourish. Nitrogen-giving trees such as acacias, being completely undisturbed, have been able to concentrate their strength on surviving and staying green, during even the worst periods of drought, when trees on other parts of the island have suffered badly through lack of water.

Below: sheer luxury in the pool
Bottom: Smilin' Harry's beach bar

4: The Southwest

All Saints – Falmouth – English Harbour and Nelson's Dockyard – Shirley Heights – Bethesda – Potworks Dam

Map on pages 50–51

For simplicity, the starting point for this route is from St John's, leaving town via Queen Elizabeth Highway, as in Route 3. The road, you will remember, joins Factory Road and leads to the abandoned Antigua Sugar Factory. Just before the sugar factory, turn right, next to a cricket field, on the road that leads to the village of Sea View Farm. However, the route joins up very simply with the previous one: if you retraced that journey to the little petrol station *(see page 58)*, and took the left turning, you would very soon reach Potworks Dam, from where you could follow this itinerary in reverse.

> **Useful markers**
> As in most parts of the island, road signs are few and far between and road numbers do not exist, so the presence of petrol stations at crossroads and corners are mentioned as they are useful markers on your journey.

SEA VIEW FARM

Sea View Farm is famous for indigenous pottery which, sadly, is almost a dying art on the island, and there are only a few potters left in the village. **Elvie's Pottery** (Mon–Sat 8am–6 pm) is on the main road, on the left. Elvie made pots here for many years, until her death in 1987, and her daughter is continuing the work. She uses local clay to fashion basic plant pots, coal pots (charcoal braziers), pitchers and candle holders.

Baked clay pots are still made at Elvie's Pottery

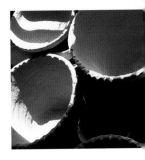

The soft clay is shaped (often with the imprints of the potter's hands) then baked in an open fire, rather than being fired in a conventional kiln. It is a small, cramped place, but visitors are welcome to stop and watch this local craft and to buy the finished products if they wish. A limited amount of the pottery is sold in the local market in St John's.

ALL SAINTS

When you reach the crossroads, after Sea View Farm, with a petrol station on the left, the main road straight ahead leads to the village of All Saints. The village gained its name because it is

Map
on pages
50–51

the central point where the parishes of St John's, St George, St Peter, St Philip's and St Mary converge. A church of 'all the saints' was constructed, houses began to spring up around it and the village was born. It is one of the larger villages on the island, prosperous looking, with a number of shops and the large white church on a corner at the traffic lights (with a petrol station on the opposite corner).

*Below: village cyclist
Bottom: the pretty church
at Tyrells*

TYRELLS

Turn right here on the main road, which leads through the village of Tyrells, and past a pretty, pink Roman Catholic church, Our Lady of Perpetual Help, built in 1932. The church is well known on the island for having a very good choir and tuneful congregation.

The village – no more than a hamlet, really – was named after Admiral Richard Tyrell who owned a sugar plantation nearby. Tyrell served as Commander-in-Chief at English Harbour in the south of the island in 1763 and died of fever at sea three years later. More recently, in 1998, the priest, Father Gerard Critch, apparently became marked with stigmata (wounds in the hands and feet, similar in appearance to those inflicted on Christ at his crucifixion) while conducting Mass.

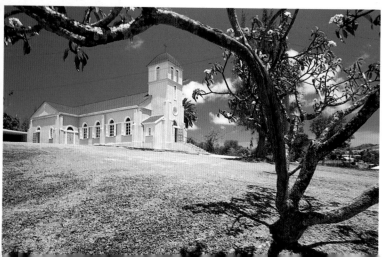

LIBERTA

Directly opposite the church, the road leads through Swetes to Fig Tree Drive *(see Route 5, page 88)*. Our journey continues on the main road to the village of **Liberta**, the first free village in Antigua and the largest on the island. In 1835, according to local records, the female estate owner 'became financially embarrassed' and had to sell much of her estate. The labourers – recently emancipated slaves – eagerly bought the land, and gave the new village its appropriate name.

GREAT GEORGE FORT

Off to the left of Liberta lie the remains of ★★ **Great George Fort**, also called Monk's Hill. To reach the site you must turn off the main road and drive to **Table Hill Gordon**. From the point where the road becomes impassable for a normal vehicle, it is a 1-mile (2-km) walk to the fort; a four-wheel-drive vehicle will take you closer. Whether on foot or on wheels, it is worth the trip to enjoy a stunning, panoramic view of the island.

THE PERFECT DETERRENT

Perched high on a hill, the site was chosen in the 1680s as the perfect location to guard Falmouth from the French, who had recently attacked St Kitts. The work was completed around 1705, but the fort was never engaged in battle. There is a stone inscription to King George II (1683–1760).

Nearly 8 acres (3 hectares) of land are surrounded by a huge stone wall and the only entrance is through an arched opening on the north side. Inside are some overgrown remains of gun sites, barracks, a hospital and water cisterns; the west powder magazine, built in 1731, has undergone some restoration. In the 19th century, after the wars with France were over, the fort became a signal station. Like many of the historic sites in Antigua, this one is in need of care and conservation. For the sure-footed, there is a path back down the other side of the hill to Cobbs Cross and Falmouth Harbour, but our route continues by road.

Star Attraction
● Great George Fort

Liberty and land
Although enslaved people were officially emancipated on 1 August 1834, many of them had no choice but to continue working on the estates. Although they were legally free, their circumstances did not change much for many years. An opportunity to purchase land – and the means to do so – was rare and represented a major step forward. For more on the history of slavery on the island, *see pages 8–9.*

Great George Fort – the views make it worth a hike

Map
on pages
50–51

FALMOUTH TOWN

Returning to the main road after the trip to Monks
Hill, keep going south for about 1 mile (2km)
towards Falmouth. From the crown of the hill,
there is a splendid view of the harbour spread
out below.

Falmouth, which grew up around the lovely
natural harbour, was the first English settlement
on the island, but the town is small and unpre-
possessing today. James Pitt, brother of England's
youngest prime minister, William, is buried in the
churchyard of St Paul's beside the main road.
He died here in 1780.

RENDEZVOUS BEACH

Before getting down to the main event, Nelson's
Dockyard, there is a diversion that could be made,
although the second half of it must be done on
foot. Take a right turn on Farrell Avenue, which
leads to Rendezvous Beach. The road soon
becomes a track fringed with banana groves and
with mango trees that drip with ripe fruit between
March and August. It is accessible by car until the
point where it passes the **Spring Hill Riding
School**, where BHS qualified instructors offer
lessons and treks *(see page 114)*.

Past the school the track becomes very bumpy
indeed and you need to continue on foot, but it's
well worth the hike (bring plenty of drinking
water). It runs between Cherry Hill and Sugar
Loaf Hill (the latter, at 1,042ft/318m, one of the
higher points on this flat island) before dropping
down to the palm-fringed turquoise waters of
★★ **Rendezvous Beach**, among the most magnificent on the island. You may share the beach
with an occasional small boat-load from Falmouth
Harbour, but there is a good chance that you will
have it all to yourself.

FALMOUTH HARBOUR

Returning to the main route – if you made the
Rendezvous Beach diversion – the road runs
along beside ★★ **Falmouth Harbour**. You will

Fresh coffee

En route to Falmouth, a
right turn down an unpaved
track leads to the Carib Coffee Bean
Company, which has been operating
here since 1997. Estate-grown
Arabica coffee beans are imported
from the Caribbean Basin, and parts
of Latin and Central America and
freshly roasted daily. This is the only
such operation on the island and the
aroma from the roasting beans let
you know that you are buying the
freshest coffee available.

Riding on the beach

pass the Catamaran Club and Jetty, one of several marinas where luxurious yachts and speedy sailing boats are moored. A walk along the jetty is fascinating for anyone interested in sailing.

The road runs through Cobbs Cross, passing the Falmouth Marina and turns right into English Harbour Town, as it's officially called, although it is no more than a village now. Another right turn will take you past the Antigua Yacht Club and several bars and restaurants, such as Jackee's Kwik Stop, which serves good local dishes. This area, which separates Falmouth and English harbours, is called Middle Ground. A narrow road continues round it to Pigeon Beach and on to Windward Bay.

Star Attractions
- **Rendezvous Beach**
- **Falmouth Harbour**
- **Nelson's Dockyard**

Below: Nelson's Dockyard
Bottom: Catamaran Club

NELSON'S DOCKYARD

The direct route takes you down the east side of Middle Ground, to ★★★ **Nelson's Dockyard** (daily 9am–5pm; entrance fee includes Shirley Heights and Dow's Hill Interpretation Centre). This is the only Georgian naval facility still in use in the world, and has been preserved and beautifully renovated as a National Park; it is worth an extended visit. You enter through a covered market area (with phones, a bank, post office and toilets) where souvenirs and crafts are on sale and you can buy freshly-squeezed fruit juice.

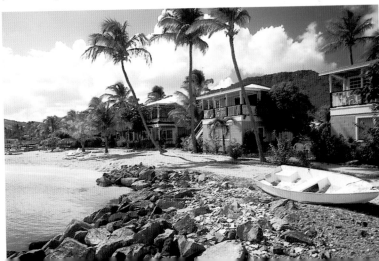

Map on pages 50–51

> **Trees in the dockyard**
> The dockyard is well planted with flowering trees and bushes, among them the lignum vitae, known as iron wood because the timber is so hard. It used to be widely used for boat building, and in the construction of sugar mills. The coconut tree (*Cocos nucifera*), which has the largest seed in the world, is also identified. Next to the Admiral's House is a tree believed to be more than 200 years old. The sandbox tree was so called because its dried pods were filled with sand and kept on the officers' desks, where they used it in place of blotting paper to dry wet ink on documents.

HISTORICAL DETAILS

The dockyard dates from 1743, although most of the preserved buildings were constructed towards the end of the 18th century. Its purpose was as a careening station, where British ships were scraped, repaired, and restocked with water and supplies. The harbour on which it sits was originally chosen as a hurricane haven in the 1670s for the ships that protected the West Indian colonies from enemy attack (from Dow's Hill Interpretation Centre at the top of the hill, *see page 71*, you will fully appreciate how completely safe and sheltered the harbour is).

Horatio Nelson (neither Lord nor Admiral at the time) was in command here from 1784 to 1787. His brief was to enforce the Navigation Acts, which prohibited direct trade between the newly independent states of America and the British colonies. He took his task so seriously that he managed to alienate everyone concerned, and his stay in mosquito-ridden English Harbour – 'this infernal spot', he once called it – was not a happy one.

By the late 19th century, steam power had taken over from sail, and the facility gradually became irrelevant, finally closing in 1889. Renovation work began in the 1950s, and the dockyard reopened in 1961. It is once again a working harbour, as well as one of Antigua's biggest tourist attractions.

EXPLORING THE DOCKYARD

The first building you come to used to be the Pitch and Tar Store, and is now a hotel and restaurant, **Admiral's Inn**, very popular with the yachting fraternity. Next you come to a rectangle of huge, brick pillars; they once formed the lower floor of the **Boat and Sail Loft**. A sail house was perched on top, and the design enabled boats' hulls to be cleaned and repaired below while the sails received attention above. The pillars have been topped off with rounded 'hats' to prevent further erosion. Beside the pillars is the **Sick House**, now an annexe of Admiral's Inn, but originally

Admiral's Inn at Nelson's Dockyard

the naval hospital. Fever was rife, and it was said that most patients didn't come out alive.

THE LIFE OF THE DOCKYARD

As you continue along the main path you will pass a number of buildings (most have helpful information boards outside) before reaching the ★★ **Admiral's House**, which is now an interesting maritime museum (same hours as dockyard), with a figurehead of Nelson over the door. A gift shop, library and research centre are also housed here. Although the house was built for the commanding officer (in 1855, long after Nelson's time), no admiral ever spent a night here. The Admiral's Kitchen, set back from the museum, is now the **Dockyard Bakery**, where freshly-baked pastries can be bought.

Below: Copper and Lumber Store
Bottom: the huge pillars of the Boat House

The original **Copper and Lumber Store**, close by, has become an attractive hotel and restaurant *(see page 125)* and the Mainbrace Pub next door is also a good place to eat.

Many of the buildings now have commercial functions: Sun Yacht Charters operates from the old Joiners' Loft, Dockyard Divers from the Old Guard House, and there is a photography shop, an art gallery, a pharmacy and Limey's Restaurant in the **Officers' Quarters**, where officers lived during the hurricane season.

Map
on pages
50–51

FORT BERKELEY

A path behind the Copper and Lumber Store leads around the dinghy dock to ★ **Fort Berkeley**, on the headland. Only ruins remain, but they are atmospheric, and well worth visiting. The guard house has been restored and the original powder magazine, which had the capacity to store 300 barrels of gunpowder, can be seen. From the fort, which was the first defensive point built to guard English Harbour, and named after Admiral James Berkeley, First Lord of the Admiralty, you get a good sense of what the whole complex was about.

Across the mouth of **Galleon Bay**, now a haven for some splendid yachts, a chain used to be stretched, to prevent small enemy boats entering the harbour. It was joined to Fort Charlotte on the far side, but the latter, destroyed by an earthquake in 1843, is now only identifiable as a pile of rubble.

Below and bottom: general views around Fort Berkeley

UP THE HILL

If you are feeling really fit and energetic you could continue up the track (turn off just before Fort Berkeley) to the sparse ruins of Keane's one-gun battery and the remains of **Fort Cuyler**, which looks south towards the French island of Guadeloupe. When it was built in 1798 by General Cuyler there were four 32-pound guns, and when

one was fired in 1799 the platform sank seven inches. There are spectacular views from here, and it does demonstrate the strategic importance of this piece of land. A poor track leads down the hill towards Pigeon Beach on the other side of Middle Ground.

CLARENCE HOUSE

From Nelson's Dockyard, a narrow road winds uphill, and a right turn leads to **Clarence House**, which has a superb situation overlooking the harbour. This used to be the residence of the governor-general of Antigua, but it fell into disrepair over the years and is now under restoration. When completed, part of it will be opened as a museum devoted to the lives of people who stayed there, from Prince William, Duke of Clarence (1765–1837), for whom it was built, to successive governors of the Leeward Islands, and the late Princess Margaret and the Earl of Snowdon, who spent their honeymoon here in 1960. The Duke of Clarence was stationed here as an officer in the British navy – he was made an admiral in 1811 – and became known as the Sailor King when he succeeded to the throne as William IV in 1830.

Dow's Hill Interpretation Centre

DOW'S HILL INTERPRETATION CENTRE

Past Clarence House a track to the left leads to the **Dow's Hill Interpretation Centre** (daily 9am–5pm; entrance fee includes the dockyard and Shirley Heights) built with the aid of a grant from the Canadian government. There is a café at the centre and a 15-minute multimedia presentation, which illustrates Antigua's history with illuminated tableaux and television screens. The tone of the commentary appears to be aimed at children, but it does provide a brief summary of the island's history, from the early days of Arawak settlement, through sugar, slavery and British military might, to independence and the present day.

The great thing about the centre is its situation. It stands among the ruins of the house built in the 18th century for General Alexander Dow,

Map on pages 50–51

Below: military ruins on the Heights
Bottom: Sunday shopping at Shirley Heights

which was destroyed by the 1843 earthquake. From the **Belvedere** the view over the dockyard, English Harbour and idyllic Galleon Bay is quite spectacular. It is also the best way to appreciate how completely hidden from view English Harbour was. There could be no better situation from which to shelter from hurricanes or to have the advantage over approaching enemy ships.

SCALING THE HEIGHTS

From the Interpretation Centre the road winds uphill along The Ridge to ★★★**Shirley Heights**. A left fork takes you to the **Blockhouse**, on top of Cape Shirley, Antigua's most southerly point. From here you look down on Eric Clapton's palatial house and grounds, and on **Indian Creek**. Along the shores here early Arawak artefacts were discovered. It is believed that Carib Indians attacked the more peaceful Arawaks at this site, plundering and burning their settlement.

Mamora Bay and the immense sweep of Willoughby Bay can also be seen from here. You can scramble down the cacti-covered hill to the creek if you are feeling adventurous.

Back on the main track, the first structure you reach is the well-preserved ruin of the **Officers' Quarters**, on the right. Opposite them is the **military cemetery**, where the many victims of yellow fever were buried. A few gravestones and memorials still stand on the blustery clifftop.

SHIRLEY HEIGHTS LOOKOUT

The road now comes to an enforced stop at the remnants of **Fort Shirley**, named after General Sir Thomas Shirley, governor of the Leeward Islands from 1781–91. The fort was built in the 1780s to protect the dockyard and harbour from French or American attack, and continued to be manned for several decades after any real military threat had passed.

One of the ordnance buildings has become ★★★**Shirley Heights Lookout**, a deservedly popular café and restaurant. There is an outdoor eating area at the back, from where the views are superlative. The Lookout is good for a meal or drink at any time, but on Sunday it is the site of one of the most lively events on the island. A huge outdoor barbecue takes over from the restaurant's kitchen, and the efficient staff work non-stop supplying the crowds of visitors and Antiguans who throng up the hill to listen to steel bands (from 3–7pm) and reggae (from 7pm onwards). The main event is a natural one – the sunset, an unforgettable sight. A Sunday visit to The Lookout is the stuff of holiday memories – as well as countless photographs.

Star Attractions
● **Shirley Heights**
● **Shirley Heights Lookout**

BATS' CAVE

Accessible both from Dow's Hill, and via a track off the Cobbs Cross to Mamora road *(see page 74)* is **Bats' Cave**, named for the thousands of bats (*Brachyphylla cavernarum*) that make their home inside and breed here in large numbers. Set in a rocky outcrop it is, in fact, a system of caves, that provide ideal conditions for these creatures.

There are several stories connected to the cave. It is believed that the Carib Indians used it and there is a myth that a tunnel ran from it, connecting Antigua and Guadeloupe underwater. The entrance is large and leads to a lower level where a passage leads deeper into the cave.

Trip to the Heights
Hotels arrange taxi or minibus trips for guests to Shirley Heights on Sunday afternoon. This is a good way of getting there even if you have a hired car, as the traffic can be very heavy and you may have to park some distance away.

Sunday afternoon at the Lookout

Map
on pages
50–51

GAINING ACCESS

You can only visit the cave if you have a letter of authorisation from the National Park Authority in Nelson's Dockyard (tel: 481 5023/5022 24 hours in advance and pick up the letter in person). You will then be given information about gaining access to the cave. It is not a site that the National Park or the tourist office are currently promoting as a visitor attraction, but it can be visited if you are interested, and go through the above formalities. Good, non-slip footwear and a torch are recommended.

Below and bottom: aspects of the exclusive St James Club

BETHESDA

Retracing your route from Shirley Heights and Dow's Hill back to Cobbs Cross on the edge of Falmouth Harbour, take the road that runs eastwards to **Mamora Bay**, on the edge of which perches the exclusive St James Club Resort. If you do not want to go this far, then turn left at the crossroads and follow the road that meanders along the coast by Willoughby Bay *(see Route 3, pages 59–60)*. It then turns slightly inland towards Christian Hill and **Bethesda**.

The biblical-sounding village got its name from one of the first schoolrooms opened in the Caribbean for the education of slaves, in May 1813. The name means 'hallowed'. Charles Thwaites, a

dockyard employee, at English Harbour, would travel with his wife to Lyon's Estate to teach the slaves – adults and children – until the couple decided it would be more convenient to build a school halfway between the two places. After emancipation in 1834, houses began to appear on the surrounding hillsides and the village was born.

SYMBOLIC TREE

On the northern outskirts of the village is the **Bethesda Tamarind tree**. It is easy to spot as it is the largest tree beside the road (on the left on a slight curve) and painted white around the base. The tree has a symbolic meaning for Antiguans. In 1951, when the Antigua Trades and Labour Union was newly formed, a number of workers on the sugar estates went on strike over rates of pay. Union leaders insisted that no work would be done until the matter was resolved, even though the employer stated that he would starve the strikers into submission.

The workers and their families suffered enormous hardships and were reduced to living off what natural resources they could harvest from land and sea, but in the end they won the dispute, despite military intervention and imprisonment for some of their leaders. In January 1952 the sugar workers were awarded a 25 percent wage increase and went back to work. The tamarind tree was the site of one of the meetings between the two sides as they attempted to thrash out their differences, and has become a symbol of the workers' struggle.

Workers stop for a well-earned break

TO POTWORKS DAM

From Bethesda the road leads around the eastern side of Potworks Dam, passing the remains of Blake's Sugar Mill on the right – although there is very little left of what was once a thriving estate. At the junction (just to the west of where the road from Betty's Hope emerges opposite the petrol station, *see page 58*) turn left and follow the road past Potworks Dam.

Map
on pages
50–51

DROUGHT RELIEF

Potswork Dam is named after an 18th-century pottery owned, like so much else on the island, by the Codrington family. It was officially opened in May 1970, after the need for it had been recognised for some time. Construction work had started in 1968, a drought year when only 24 inches (60cm) of rain fell, well below the annual average of 44 inches (111cm). However, the dam was barely finished when heavy rains filled the reservoir to capacity, proving that the weather here can be capricious. It is an enormous freshwater catchment, reputedly the largest in the Eastern Caribbean. It is 1 mile (2km) long and half a mile (1km) wide, and has a capacity for 1 billion gallons (4.5 billion litres) of water.

During several periods of severe drought Potswork has been a life-saver. Shortage of water is a problem on Antigua, one which means that much agricultural land is not being fully utilised and the island cannot be self-sufficient in terms of fresh produce, some of which has to be imported from neighbouring islands.

Birds
Some 150 species of birds have been recorded in Antigua and Barbuda, either residents or migrants making regular stop-overs. The offshore islands, mangrove lagoons and reservoirs such as Potsworks provide constant interest; but there are birds such as the banaquit, the Lesser Antillean bullfinch and the Antillean crested hummingbird that can be seen without leaving the grounds of your hotel.

BIRDWATCHING

The area attracts a wonderful variety of birdlife and is of great interest to birdwatchers, especially around the western edge. Among the birds seen here are the osprey *(Pandion haliaetus)* the snowy egret *(Egretta thula)* and the West Indian whistling duck *(Dendrocygna arborea)*.

The cattle egret *(Bubulcus ibis)* is also a common sight. This bird can be seen all over the island, standing patiently beside a cow and cleaning the animal's hide of insects, as well as devouring any creatures that the cow's movements disturb from the earth.

Leaving the dam, follow the road until it joins the main route back to St John's, passing the Antigua Sugar Factory and entering town via Queen Elizabeth Highway. If you are heading back towards the Dickenson Bay area, take the same road, then turn right onto Factory Road, then right by the Recreation Ground to go north.

Potworks Dam has done a lot to alleviate drought

5: The West Coast

Five Islands – Fort Barrington – Jolly Harbour – Boggy Peak – Old Road – Fig Tree Drive – Wallings Conservation Project – Claremont Pineapple Farm – Swetes

Map
on pages
50–51

The west coast is the lushest and loveliest part of the island, and the area with the most elevated ground – Boggy Peak is the highest point. The route begins on the peninsula between the harbours of St John's and Five Islands, an area of noticeable contrasts. Once again, for simplicity's sake, we begin at the junction of Independence Drive and Queen Elizabeth Highway.

Below: roadside shack menu
Bottom: misty view from Boggy Peak

FIVE ISLANDS

Travel south out of town down Independence Drive and bear right on Viv Richards Street (the one-way system will leave you little alternative if you want to go south). At the traffic lights cross over Valley Road and go straight ahead on the road alongside St John's Harbour, crossing a narrow strip of reclaimed land.

A left turn leads to **Five Islands Village**, named after five tiny, rocky islands at the other side of the eponymous harbour. This is a large and lively village with plenty of small shops and bar shacks and neatly-dressed children on their way to and

Map on pages 50–51

from school, but poverty is evident. There was apparently no settlement here at all at the time of emancipation (1834), but by 1842 a village had grown up around a **Moravian church**. The church that stands today, as you approach the village, is an imposing one.

Turn left when you reach it and drive through the village (a right turn would take you on a more bumpy and circuitous track). At a T-junction, opposite the Faith Supermarket, turn right on the main road. At the next junction you will pass an abandoned sugar mill, on a hillock to your right, as the road wends its way past brackish ponds (with some good birdlife), a number of charcoal burning pits, and herds of goats grazing beside them – and wandering into the road at will.

Below: smiling for the camera
Bottom: shady arbour at Galley Bay

CHARCOAL BURNING

Charcoal burning is a traditional Antiguan practice that still flourishes today. Records show that, in 1990, 112 people were employed full time in this trade and some 1,200 tons of charcoal were produced. Tree branches (preferably *Acacia nilotica*) are buried in the earth and burned to produce a hard charcoal that is longer burning than commercial coal and therefore more economical as a source of fuel for cooking.

GALLEY BAY

To reach Galley Bay, follow numerous signs to Chez Pascal then turn right at a larger-than-usual one ('Exquisite, Don't Miss It') and drive past a salt pond where pelicans and white herons put on a regular show. There is a small island in the centre, and a bridge leading across to it.

Leave your car by the Galley Bay Hotel (where a sign says '*five minutes' walk to Chez Pascal*') and walk up a gradual hill past a collection of pretty chalets belonging to Galley Bay resort, where herons come almost down to the path to greet you.

★ **Chez Pascal**, at the top, is a delightful (but expensive) French restaurant set in flowery, landscaped grounds with a small pool *(see page 110)*. Even if you are not eating here, stop for a drink and to admire the magnificent view of Galley Bay, Deep Bay, St John's Harbour and beyond, and to spot the wreck of the *Andes*, a cargo ship that sank in 1905, lying in only 20ft (6m) of water in Deep Bay. Because it is so shallow, the wreck makes an excellent snorkelling site.

> **Wreck of the *Andes***
> The *Andes*, a British sailing ship registered in Hull, Yorkshire, in 1874, caught fire in St John's Harbour in June 1905 while she was carrying 1,330 barrels of pitch from Trinidad to Valparaiso. The wreck was towed to Deep Bay, so that it did not obstruct the harbour.

HAWKSBILL ROCK

Rejoin the road now and turn right; keep going a short distance until you reach the imposing stone gates that form the entrance to the **Hawksbill Hotel**. Non-residents are welcome. It is a serene, attractive place, with villas and apartments set out in luxuriant grounds. There's a small pool and several pretty beaches with sea kayaks lying invitingly on the white sands. From the beaches you can see, about half a mile (1km) offshore, the **Hawksbill Rock** from which the complex took its name. The large rock does, in fact, look very much like the head of a hawksbill sea turtle.

SIR GEORGE'S OLD BATTERY

If you fancy a hike, the ruins of **Sir George's Old Battery** are on Fullerton Point to the south, but they are not easy to reach. The battery is prominently shown on maps of Antigua, but little remains. The location is impressive, though.

Hawksbill – windsurfing past the aptly-named rock

Map
on pages
50–51

ROYAL ANTIGUAN

Drive back past the Chez Pascal turning and the salt pond, until you reach a T-junction where there is a blue bus shelter and two phone boxes. Turn left here, passing a primary school (painted with a pink wash, like all the primary schools on the island) where children share their playing field with a few munching goats. You will soon arrive at the gates of the Royal Antiguan Hotel. From the outside, it is a rather unappealing, nine-storey concrete structure, but it has all the facilities a visitor could ask for and it is set right on the beach edging the lovely **Deep Bay**.

Drive around the hotel's well-made-up road (it looks private but it isn't) and when you reach the exit turn sharp left down a track signed to Ocean Grill and Trafalgar Villas. The track forks after a few hundred yards/metres; take the left fork to the sea, where a narrow pedestrian bridge leads across an estuary to **Goats' Hill**.

Signal station

Signals from Fort Barrington were sent to Rat Island, overlooking St John's, or sometimes to Monk's Hill in the south of the island. In the 1843 *Antigua Almanac* a complete list of signals are given, such as No. 456, 'Boat Upset on Sandy Island', and No. 534 'Suspicious Sail to the South'. The fort continued to act as a signalling station, reporting the arrival of ships for the Harbour Department until the early 1960s.

FORT BARRINGTON

It's a steep but short scramble up the footpath to the circular remains of ★★ **Fort Barrington** on the top of the little hill. The first fort was built here in the 1650s to guard St John's Harbour. Fort James *(see page 33)*, begun a couple of decades later, stood guard on the other side. Barrington was captured by the French in 1666 when they took St John's, but returned to the British the following year under the Treaty of Breda.

Relative peace reigned for more than a century but in 1779, when the French were once more seen as a serious threat, it was heavily fortified by Admiral Barrington, who had defeated the French off St Lucia the previous year. In 1790 the fortress was strengthened once again, but saw no military action. Once the threat of attack was deemed to have receded Barrington, like Great George Fort *(see page 65)* became a signal station, reporting on the movement of ships in the vicinity.

The ruins are redolent of the island's maritime history, and the views from this lonely spot are spectacular, especially at sunset.

Steep steps at Fort Barrington

HEADING SOUTH

Return to the road by the Royal Antiguan exit and follow it round a little bay where refreshment shacks line a rather scruffy little beach, until it joins the main road, with Jolly Harbour sign-posted to the left. Follow it a short distance back to the Valley Road junction on the outskirts of St John's and turn right at the traffic lights. Drive past a few stalls selling fruit and vegetables, snacks and drinks; where the road divides, take the right-hand fork (at another pink primary school), which leads through the villages of Golden Grove and Creekside and crosses the bright yellow Creekside Bridge.

GREEN CASTLE HILL

Just after the bridge a track leads off to the left, towards ★ **Green Castle Hill** and Emanuel village. Drive to the village and start your walk to the top of the hill by the gates of a brick factory, off to the right, near a stone quarry. The climb takes about 45 minutes, but it is not particularly steep or difficult and the views from the top make it well worth the effort.

The 565-ft (172-m) grassy hill is the remnant of an isolated volcano. There are large rocks and boulders, so-called megaliths, scattered around the south-western summit of the hill, which some

Star Attraction
● Fort Barrington

Below: goats on Goat Hill
Bottom: the view from the fort over Deep Bay

like to associate with ancient pagan rites, although there is no evidence to back this up.

BELOVED GOVERNOR

There is also a large stone plaque at one end of the summit, commemorating Lord Baldwin, Governor of the Leeward Islands from 1947–49, whose ashes are buried beneath it. He left Antigua for England when his term of office ended but when he died in 1958 his ashes were returned to the island, in accordance with his wishes, and interred here, as two steel bands played.

Below: travelling salesman
Bottom: colourful Chinese restaurant

This charismatic governor was responsible for a number of social reforms and did much to pave the way for independence. He endeared himself to the people of Antigua and reciprocated their affection. An inscription on the plaque reads: 'He loved the people of these islands'.

EBENEZER AND JENNINGS

The road south continues through the village of **Ebenezer**, from where the 87-ft (26-m) red and white Cable & Wireless communication tower can be seen on the top of Boggy Peak *(see page 87)*. The next village is **Jennings**, which began as a small estate owned, in 1749, by Samuel Jennings. Later in the 18th century it passed into the

hands of the ever-acquisitive Codrington family, but by the time of emancipation in 1834 it had changed ownership again. The Moravian church then established a school here and the village of Jennings sprang up around it.

SIMPLE PLEASURES

One of the greatest pleasures of driving through these villages, and many others around the island, is not the major sites you will discover, but the chance to see how the ordinary people of Antigua live. Strung out along the main (often the only) road are brightly-painted wooden houses, known as chattel houses, a term left over from the days of slavery. In season they are smothered with bougainvillaea, hibiscus and other bright blossoms, while banana palms give shade outside.

Sometimes you have to look closely to distinguish between a house, a shop and a bar. Then you will see small signs that tell you that one is the A–B Grocery Store, another is Jean's Snackette, Angel's Beauty Parlour or the Hi-Life Video Store, and a bright pink structure, bigger than some of the others, will be identified as the Dragon Phoenix Chinese Restaurant.

Children, immaculate in crisp uniforms and snowy-white socks throng the pavements at the end of the school day. On Sunday, people file into the numerous churches of all denominations, men in smart suits, women wearing colourful dresses and elegant hats, and clutching bibles.

You will see roadside vendors, some roasting sweetcorn, others with bags of nuts or a few cold drinks. An elderly lady in a bright headscarf and with a lap full of grandchildren may have some mangos or a pile of bananas for sale.

You may get held up, briefly, behind a flat-back truck, dropping off labourers at their places of work; or stuck for a while behind a rickety food waggon with a sign announcing that it sells 'Pizza and Tings'. And everywhere you go, the goats that graze on every bit of open land will wander into the road whenever they think the grass looks greener on the other side.

Caribbean Lighthouse
On the road between Jennings and Bolans you pass a little dolls' house of a radio station, the Caribbean Lighthouse Radio, with a small lighthouse outside. Funded by the Baptist International Mission in Chattanooga, and staffed by a small team of committed Baptists, some of them American student volunteers, their mission is to broadcast religious programmes and music to the islands, and beyond.

Coming home from school

Map
on pages
50–51

*Below: quiet life at Cocobay
Bottom: lovely Darkwood Beach*

PEARNS POINT

Just outside Jennings a right turn leads to the westernmost point of Antigua, Pearns Point. The road – which is not a good one, and is best travelled in a four-wheel-drive vehicle – passes York's Village, the remains of York's Sugar Mill and the ruins of an estate house. There are two beautiful and very isolated beaches here, in Hermitage Bay and Pearns Bay. The former has been the site of a royal dip off the royal yacht when Queen Elizabeth has paid official state visits to the island. There are two salt ponds, as well, Yorks and Jolly Hill, with a good variety of birdlife. But be warned, there is also a bay called Mosquito Cove.

JOLLY GOOD FUN

Back on the main route, the landscape opens up and, after there has been some rain, becomes pleasantly verdant. A series of conical, wooded hills and, beyond, some lofty palm trees, announce that you are approaching the coast. The road passes the Christian Valley Agricultural Station on the left, the tiny Caribbean Lighthouse Radio Station *(see page 83)* on the right, and a cheerful red-and-white refreshment stand called Rainbow's End, before reaching **Bolans** village and the large Jolly Beach Resort and Jolly Harbour complexes.

The two Jollies initially share a driveway but you go straight ahead for Jolly Beach, an all-inclusive resort hotel spread along an idyllic beach on Lignumn Vitae Bay (named after the hardwood tree); and turn right for Jolly Habour. The latter has a sheltered harbour and a smart marina, an 18-hole golf course, a casino and its own helipad, set among the villas and apartments for sale and rent.

VALLEY CHURCH

The main road then passes the picturesque, red-roofed **Our Lady of the Valley** church, which stands opposite a mangrove pond. Here the antics of pelicans, egrets, and noisy, long-legged avocets, locally known as darling birds, can provide hours of entertainment from the road, or more comfortably from **Valley Church Beach**.

The beach lies beyond the mangroves, separated by a neatly-tended expanse of grass. Newly laid vehicle paths from the road to the beach suggest that it may become more developed in the near future.

On a bluff sit the pretty pink and turquoise villas of **Cocobay Resort**, followed by a succession of gorgeous white beaches. **Ffryes Bay** is very popular with locals and visitors. It offers plenty of shade and parking and is an ideal spot for a picnic or barbecue.

DARKWOOD BEACH

★★**Darkwood Beach**, which is the next one round, is regarded by many as the best beach on Antigua, but with 365 beaches to choose from, this is often debated. The only development is a beach bar and restaurant which has been here since 1975, making it the oldest beach bar on the island. It is family-owned and operated; Clyde George carved the site out of bush and has completely rebuilt it twice, after damage by Hurricane Luís in 1995 and again by Hurricane Lenny in 1999. From Darkwood Beach, and several other spots along here, you can see the neighbouring island of Montserrat.

Star Attraction
● Darkwood Beach

 Orange Valley
From Cocobay Resort, guided walks through an area known as Orange Valley can be arranged. This is an old plantation estate that is rich in indigenous species. Your guide will be a botanist, who cultivates aloe vera on the estate, and will point out medicinal plants and talk about their uses as you go along. For information or to arrange a walk, tel: 562 2400.

The splash pool and beach bar at Jolly Beach Resort

Map
on pages
50–51

SUNSET AT TURNER'S BEACH

★ **Turner's Beach** is lively, with seafood restaurants (lobster a speciality) and local art for sale in a shop across the road. Turner's Rudder Beach Bar, in a pink and green chattel house, is a busy spot during the season.

*Below: Turner's Beach Bar
Bottom: chattel houses
at Old Road*

On Sunday afternoon, the **Heavenly Hill Gallery** (1–7pm; tel: 560 1245) runs a 'sunset over Montserrat' afternoon, with displays of work by local artists and South African wine tastings. There is a sign to it just south of the beach, near Pelican Villas.

REEFS AND PINEAPPLES

The drive continues through the busy little village of **Urlings**, which is a flourishing fishing community, and passes **Cades Reef**, the longest reef on the island, that ensures calm waters for swimmers and is great for snorkelling. You will notice black pineapples, the national fruit of Antigua, for sale on stalls along the road. These fruit, which are unique to the island, are grown at nearby **Cadesby Pineapple Farm**.

You can see the plantations from the road, and the interesting thing about these pineapples – apart from their colour and especially sweet taste – is that they grow at ground level, with the palm-like fronds sitting on the soil.

Another large-scale producer, Claremont Pineapple Farm on Fig Tree Drive *(see page 88)* organises tours and tastings.

BOGGY PEAK

From Cades Bay, a road leads towards ★★ **Boggy Peak**, the highest point of the island, at 1,319ft (402m), a part of the Shekerley Mountain range. As already mentioned, the Cable & Wireless Microwave Communication System is located on the peak, secured by high fencing. For access to the area, which does offer the best views of almost the whole of the island, as well as Montserrat, St Kitts and Guadeloupe, contact Cable & Wireless (tel: 480 4000/4415). If you can't organise it, don't worry, the views from outside the fenced area are pretty stunning, too.

CURTAIN BLUFF AND OLD ROAD

On the far side of shallow Morris Bay, the exclusive **Curtain Bluff Hotel** *(see page 126)* stands out. One of the most expensive hotels on the island, it has an enviable position, as there are calm and peaceful waters on one side of the bluff, and good surfing waves on the other.

Next on the route is ★ **Old Road**, the oldest village on the island, and one of the liveliest. The original settlers of 1632 recognised the advantages of the deep sheltered Carlisle Bay, on which it sits, as it provided them with anchorage safe from storms and pirate attacks ('road' was a nautical term for anchorage). St Mary's church here is the oldest on the island.

The landscape along this stretch of coast has now become far more green and fertile, and the village is a mass of tumbling bougainvillaea, frangipani and poinsettias, as well as bananas and giant ferns. Keep your eyes open as you travel along for a huge, hollow-trunked silk cotton (kapok) tree *(Ceiba pentandra)*. You may also notice people selling huge conch shells on roadside stalls, along with black pineapples and tropical juice drinks.

Star Attraction
● Boggy Peak

Eruption on Montserrat
The 1995 volcanic eruption on Montserrat was experienced from a distance by the people of Antigua. From the western part of the island plumes of smoke could be seen, and volcanic ash blew as far afield as St John's.

Communing with the waves at Curtain Bluff

Map
on pages
50–51

FIG TREE DRIVE

From the village, the road now turns inland and winds through what is known as ★★ **Fig Tree Drive**. The first thing to remember is that there are no figs – it is an Antiguan word for bananas. And there are plenty of bananas along here, as well as mangos, guavas and soursops *(see box)*.

Near the beginning of the drive you will see **Claremont Pineapple Farm**, where tours can be taken if they are arranged in advance (tel: 462 8530 or e-mail: info@claremontfarms.com).

Simply driving along the road will give you a taste of this magnificent area of the island, and the only part that is mountainous and covered in truly tropical vegetation. But to really appreciate the riches of the region, you need to get off the road and start walking.

Soursop

Soursop is a large green fruit with prickly skin. They can be as much as 8 inches (20cm) long and weigh up to 6lbs (nearly 3kg). Although the fruit may be eaten raw, it is more often made into soft drinks, mousse and ice cream. The drinks tend to be over-sweetened, but the mousse and ice cream are delicious.

Lush foliage on Fig Tree Drive

WALLINGS FOREST RESERVE

In order to explore the ★★★ **Wallings Forest Reserve** you have to organise a visit in advance with the Forestry Unit of the Ministry of Agriculture (tel: 462 1007), whose office stands on the corner of Temple and Nevis streets in St John's. There is also an efficient private company that arranges tours, in conjunction with the unit *(see page 114 for more details)*.

The entrance to the reserve is at present signalled only by a small sign, a red and yellow stall selling drinks, fruit and the ubiquitous sarongs, and a little blue shack. The latter, however, is about to be converted into an interpretation centre, with toilets and other facilities.

FOREST LORE

At the convergence of three watersheds, the forest surrounds a reservoir, a marvellous bit of Victorian engineering, begun in 1890 and completed about a decade later. It was built to hold 13 million gallons (59 million litres) of water, enough to supply 15 villages, but when it emptied in 1912, after three years of drought, it was decided that radical action had to be taken.

The solution was to plant trees on 13 acres (5 hectares) of surrounding land, to anchor the productive top soil and enable the ground to store, and gradually release, water. This was the most important reforestation project ever undertaken on the island. Wallings is the largest tract of forest in Antigua, and the best example of the moist, evergreen forests that covered the island before they were cleared by the Europeans for sugar cane production three centuries ago.

Star Attractions
- **Fig Tree Drive**
- **Wallings Forest Reserve**

Below and bottom: mango tree and passion fruit at Claremont Pineapple Farm

VEGETATION

The three forest trails will lead you through a wide variety of vegetation. There are silk cotton trees *(Ceiba pentandra)*, so named for the material they produce, which we know as kapok. It was once used to stuff mattresses and pillows, and was also utilised for making lifebelts in both world wars. Hog plum trees *(Spondias momblin)* are plentiful; the fruits smell delicious but are regarded as an acquired taste. Quite the opposite applies to the locust trees *(Hymenaea courbaril)*, whose leathery-skinned fruit, when broken open, smells so bad that it is nicknamed 'stinking toe' – but if you hold your nose, the taste is good.

There are lots of juicy mangos, too, which fall from the trees when ripe (May–June), white cedars *(Tabebuia pallida)* and mahogany trees

Map
on pages
50–51

(*Swietenia mohogani*), although the latter do not grow to great heights here.

The summits are sweet with the scent of bright green lemon grass; there are orchids in the undergrowth, and a vine with abundant lilac-coloured flowers that tangles itself around trees and bushes.

In parts of the forest there used to be little daylight and few glimpses of the sky, but Hurricane Luís, which caused so much damage throughout the island in 1995, destroyed the canopy.

Track to the beach
There is a steep track that leads from Wallings Forest Reserve down to the beautiful Rendezvous Beach. At present the path is not well cleared or marked, although there are plans to develop it in the near future. Your guide will tell you if it is safe to use.

ANIMAL LIFE

As you would expect, there are a number of birds in the forest. You may see the Antillean crested hummingbird, both the purple- and green-throated caribs and the Lesser Antillean bullfinch.

If it has rained when you visit you will certainly hear – although you may not see – tree frogs. They are tiny, but extremely vocal. You will probably see a mongoose or two, and may be surprised to spot hermit crabs on the paths.

Curtley Ambrose and teammates celebrate. Ambrose was born in Swetes

REWARDING VIEWS

One of the three designated trails (the Forestry Unit provides useful explanatory leaflets, as well as qualified guides) will take you to a summit from where visitors can get a spectacular view over Antigua, uninhabited little Redonda, to the west, and Montserrat. Once there you will almost certainly be glad you made the effort.

Back on the road, you will pass first through little John Hughes village, and then the village of **Swetes**. The latter's chief claim to fame is as the birthplace of the former West Indies fast bowler, Curtley Ambrose. Off to the left between the two villages, a path leads to Body Ponds, a series of dammed ponds where some peaceful walks can be enjoyed.

Our route ends here; the return to St John's can be made by continuing to All Saints. Here you can take a left turn on All Saints Road, which will bring you into town to the south of Heritage Market and the West Bus Station.

6: Barbuda

A trip to the tiny neighbouring island of Barbuda is an essential part of a visit to Antigua. If the larger island can sometimes get busy in the summer months, its small, northerly neighbour provides welcome relief with tranquil, empty beaches and a leisurely pace of life.

Map on page 91

ISLAND HISTORY

The island has a rich and colourful history. The wealthy Codrington family was granted a lease

ROUTE 6
BARBUDA

0   2 miles
0   2 km

N

Goat Pt
Billy Pt
Goat Island
Kid Island
Hog Pt
Cedar Tree Pt
Rabbit Island
Indian Cave (petroglyphs)
Two Foot Bay
Codrington Lagoon
Frigate Bird Sanctuary
Rubbish Bay
Palm Beach
Darby Cave
Low Bay
Dark Cave
Codrington
Barbuda
The Highlands
Castle Bay
Welsh Pt
Martello Tower
The River Landing
Pelican Pt
Palmetto Pt
K-Club Resort
Castle (ruins)
Coco Point Beach Resort
Airstrip
Gravenour Bay
Spanish Pt
Coco Pt

CARIBBEAN SEA

Map on page 91

on the island by King Charles II in 1677, for the rent of "one fat sheep". They retained the lease for almost 200 years, although they lived in Gloucestershire while trusted "attorneys" managed their estates in the Caribbean.

The Codringtons were already established as planters in Barbados when the lease was granted and at the height of the slave and sugar trade in the 18th century they had nine plantations in all. Sir Christopher Codrington, Oxford scholar and soldier, was Governor General of the Leeward Islands from 1700 to 1704 and endowed Codrington College in Barbados.

Barbuda, however, was unsuitable for growing sugar cane, as there was neither the soil nor the water. This meant that the enslaved Africans the Codringtons brought to the island were said to have had an easier life than those condemned to the harsh labour of sugar plantations. They worked mainly as hunters, herders, farmers and fishermen, and many became skilled craftsmen. The farming background has left a legacy in place names such as Goat Island, Hog Point and Kid Island, although this does not account for Rubbish Bay.

Shameful history
The Codrington papers, documents illustrating the history of slavery in the Caribbean region, were bought by the Antiguan government at a Sotheby's auction in December 1980.

MAKING THE TRIP

It's a short hop by air to Codrington Airport

Barbuda is about 62 sq miles (160 sq km) in area, and lies some 30 miles (48km) northeast of

Antigua. Getting there is simple, if a little costly, and the best of Barbuda can be explored on a day trip. Carib Aviation and LIAT both operate regular flights, and there are several reliable private charter companies that also make the short hop.

A catamaran called the *Excellence*, makes regular sea crossings, and several other boats also take visitors to Barbuda on day trips. These usually include lunch, a visit to the frigate bird sanctuary and other points of interest, and time to swim and snorkel. *(See page 117 for details of trips)*.

Most people come to this tiny, peaceful place to visit the bird sanctuary or to enjoy miles of empty beaches, lapped by the Caribbean Sea. One of Barbuda's main attractions is a magnificent pink sand beach, that gets its colour from the compacted shells of tiny pink crustaceans.

CODRINGTON

Visitors arriving by air fly in to Codrington Airport, which is just minutes from the heart of the island capital, **Codrington**, a sleepy little town, named after the original English landholders. Most of the island's 1,500 people live here. The town has narrow streets lined with brightly coloured wooden houses, and is easy to negotiate on foot. Madison Square is the hub, the site of public meetings, political events, and a magnet for local people who come here to chill out and chat on warm evenings.

Across from the square is the Island Chalet Guest House, one of the few accommodation options for visitors on a budget *(see page 127)*.

The village well, where people gathered to draw buckets of fresh water, was in use until the late 1970s, and is still a landmark. There is a little Pentecostal Church, a few shops and bars, and not very much else.

FRIGATE BIRD SANCTUARY

The largest nesting colony of frigate birds *(Fregata magnificens)* in the world – larger even than the Galapagos colony – is located just west of

Below: an old well in Codrington
Bottom: Pilgrim Holiness Church

Map on page 91

town on the 8-mile (13-km) long **Codrington Lagoon**. The ★★★ **Frigate Bird Sanctuary** is a valuable asset to the island, and residents appreciate this, and offer a warm welcome to guests. The people who help manage the site are well trained and, in most cases, have been involved with the colony for years. They, understandably, regard it with great pride.

A leaflet providing information about the birds is available at the airport and can also be picked up at the Lagoon Wharf. Plans are underway to build an interpretative centre to provide more in-depth education and information, both on the birds, which have been extensively studied, and on the whole mangrove area.

Lobster in the lagoon
You will find plenty of fresh lobster on the menus in Barbuda. They live in the 12-mile (20-km) Codrington Lagoon and are an island delicacy. A lobster lunch is usually included as part of a day trip to the island.

ORGANISED VISITS

The colony is located at the north end of Codrington Lagoon and is home to 4,000 birds. Visitors can reach the site on private cruise boats from Antigua, or can be taken there in local open boats, which hold a maximum of 12 people. The boats motor for approximately 45 minutes through the calm lagoon, which is surrounded by thick mangroves. The birds' nesting area is staked out with a roped 10-ft (3-m) border which provides protection for the birds and prevents any intrusion on the nests, which are only a few feet from the water's edge.

Bird-watching on the lagoon

FACTS ON THE COLONY

Frigate birds (also called 'man o' war birds') actually consist of five different species and are among the oldest-known birds on the planet. Mating takes place between September and January, and both males and females share the work of nest building and incubating the egg, which hatches about 60 days after laying. Only one chick per pair is hatched, and it remains in the nest for eight to 10 months, one of the longest dependency periods of any bird species. Because of this, they only breed every other year, which is most unusual in the bird world.

During the mating season the male displays his bulbous scarlet throat sac, which attracts the attention of the female, and a fascinating courtship ritual is then played out. It is a very special experience to be so close to these birds and observe their behaviour.

On the sea-side of the lagoon, ★★★ **Palm Beach** is a magnificent 12-mile (20-km) sweep of sand, snowy white in places, pink in others.

MARTELLO TOWER

About 3 miles (5km) from Codrington, the 56-ft (17-m) ★ **Martello Tower** is the most intact part of the ruins of the River Fort. It is abandoned at present, but it is hoped that it will eventually become the island museum.

The style of Martello towers was copied from the original at Cape Martello in Corsica. Their efficacy was discovered during an attack on Corsica by the English fleet in 1794. They landed 1,400 troops, and when the tower's garrison of just 33 men finally surrendered, it was discovered that the only armaments were two 18-pound and one 6-pound guns. The British realised the Martello towers were valuable structures, and built copies along the south coast of England for defensive purposes during the Napoleonic Wars, and in their colonies, such as Barbuda.

Star Attractions
● **Frigate Bird Sanctuary**
● **Palm Beach**

Below: guide at the sanctuary
Bottom: the Martello Tower

Map
on page
91

Close to the tower is the River Landing, where boats carrying sand and lobsters (Barbuda's two main exports) to Antigua, as well as passenger ferries to and from St John's, load and unload.

SPANISH POINT

Below: look-out point in the Martello Tower
Bottom: White Bay Beach

Leaving the tower head for ★★ **Spanish Point**, a place that visitors to Barbuda should not miss. It is at the southeastern tip of the island and is the site of a magnificent beach. En route you will pass two exclusive and up-market resorts – K Club and Coco Point *(see page 127)*. Guests are flown from Antigua to the small airstrip that lies between the two.

At Spanish Point is one of the most beautiful beaches imaginable – ★★ **White Bay Beach**. It is also the stepping-off point for the **Palaster Reef**, where there is excellent snorkelling and scuba diving. The reef has been a marine reserve since 1972, and offers exciting underwater exploration, but the area is strictly protected by law, so collecting shells or coral, and any kind of fishing (including spear fishing), is prohibited.

Palaster Reef has caused a number of shipwrecks over the centuries. The British warship, HMS *Griffin*, built in 1758, met her fate on this reef, and at least 57 other ships have been wrecked around the waters of Barbuda. Disastrous for the

poor mariners, but for the shipwreck diver, this place is a paradise.

Just to the east of Spanish Point, shown on most maps as The Castle, the sparse ruins of what was a lookout tower, for defence against attacks by Carib Indians, remain. Its strategic position means that it offers a fabulous view.

Star Attractions
- ● **Spanish Point**
- ● **White Bay Beach**
- ● **Darby's Cave**

THE HIGHLANDS

On the north side of the island lies an area called the Highlands – although they are not very high. There is little development and the land is wilder. Here, the fallow deer that the Codringtons introduced roam freely, along with wild boar, genie hens, ducks and whistling ducks. There are legal hunting seasons for the various kinds of game.

What limited agriculture there is on Barbuda – sweet potatoes, peanuts and peas, mainly – will be found here, too. Otherwise, the terrain is scrubby and rather bare. There are several caves in the area; none of them should be explored alone, but it is easy to arrange for a guide.

Scrubby terrain on the Highlands

DARBY'S CAVE

★★ **Darby's Cave**, a sinkhole not far from Rubbish Bay, is reached via a (driveable) dirt track from Codrington, then a 40-minute trek with a guide. The sinkhole has vertical, cliff-like sides and is around 70ft (22m) deep and 300ft (92m) in diameter. It is surrounded by lush vegetation and a number of tall trees grow in the cave, with their tops at eye level. The only specimen of the rare Mari tree *(Calophyllum antillanum)* on the island grows here.

The path drops precipitously and sunlight filters through the trees and vegetation. There is an abundance of bird life in the dark interior, which resembles a tropical rainforest. A 30-ft (9-m) overhanging cliff has formed stalagmites of calcium carbonate.

There are a number of sink holes in the Highlands, but Darby's is the most notable. Carbon dioxide from the air and decaying organic matter

Map on page 91

forms carbonic acid which erodes soluble sedimentary rock, such as limestone. As the rocks dissolve, they become honeycombed with caverns. If they are close to the surface of the earth, the roof may collapse, forming a sink hole.

DARK CAVE

★★ **Dark Cave** is in the middle of the Highlands about 4 miles (7km) east of Codrington, and just south of Darby's Sinkhole. The cave has a low entrance on the north side of a shallow sinkhole and the access is through a narrow slit. To reach the large cavern – about 300ft (92m) long and 60ft (18m) wide – visitors have to crawl, so it is not for the claustrophobic. The descent continues about 400ft (122m) through a difficult passage, passing huge boulders and overhangs. On reaching the bottom you find several connected chambers and a series of five freshwater pools stretching away into the darkness.

Two Foot Bay
It is said that Two Foot Bay got its name after an escaping slave ran with his shoes on backwards to fool his pursuers.

RARE SPECIES

The rare blind shrimps (*Typhlatya monae*) are found in these pools. They are only otherwise known to exist on Mona Island, off Hispaniola. Amphipods, another crustacean, found nowhere else in the world, also inhabit the water. Near the entrance to the cave, seafood remains and pottery shards have been unearthed, indicating that there was an Amerindian settlement here. It is believed that this settlement dates from about AD800. Traces of Arawak Indian sites have also been found at Spanish Point and at Two Foot Bay.

Rough seas at Spanish Point

INDIAN CAVE

★★ **Indian Cave**, the most interesting prehistoric site on Barbuda, is located at Two Foot Bay (*see box*) on the northeast coast. The small entrance is through a series of caverns which lead directly to a round chamber called the Drop Cavern. This is connected to the Bat Chamber, a 35-ft (10-m) cavern where numerous bats live. From the main entrance there is a short, narrow passage and two small Amerindian petroglyphs (rock drawings) can be seen as the passage opens into another cave where daylight filters in. The Amerindian people used rock drawings to guard their caves and the people in them from evil spirits. These are the only ones known to exist in Antigua or Barbuda.

It is believed that Indian Cave was the look-out for a large Amerindian site that lay not far away. Some years ago a valuable artefact was found at this site – a stone 'dog's head' with a Y-shaped hole in it. Shamans would have used this to smoke narcotics, by placing their nostrils at the top of the Y. Unfortunately, it can't be seen here: it is now part of a valuable collection of Lesser Antillean Amerindian artefacts in a New York City museum.

HIGHLAND HOUSE

The highest point on this flat island, about 3 miles (5km) from Codrington, is just 120ft (37m). The ruins of **Highland House** (known locally as Willybob) can be found here. The house was built at William Codrington's request in the 1720s, and the overgrown remains of the stables, a water cistern and part of an aqueduct are still visible. The most interesting thing about the place, however, is the view, which is quite spectacular.

Star Attractions
● Dark Cave
● Indian Cave

Below and bottom: no one's too young, or too old, to play on the beach

Cultured rivalry

Physically and politically, there are dissimilarities between Antigua and Barbuda. The gently undulating Antiguan hills offer a distinctly different landscape from the low-lying coral atoll of Barbuda. The two islands are uneasy political associates, too, as the distinctive cultural pride of Barbudans fiercely underpins calls for greater autonomy from the bigger sister island. Yet there is more that unites than divides them. As well as the vestiges of a British colonial past, both islands share a lively patois, a vibrant Carnival tradition, and long established, animated music and sporting occasions. The advent of tourism has undoubtedly encouraged the latter, and boosted special events such as the annual Sailing Week.

Opposite: infectious steel band music
Below: Viv Richards, a national hero
Bottom: adoring cricket fans

CRICKET

Cricket was introduced by the British in the early 19th century and remained an élite game for many years, but was taken up and perfected by sugar plantation workers. The Rising Sun Cricket Club in St John's was the first to be established for working-class people, in 1920.

Living legend and 'Master Blaster', Sir Isaac Vivian Alexander Richards, is worshipped as the greatest local hero. He captained the West Indies XI during some of their finest years and scored the fastest test century on his home ground against England in 1986. Before him, batsman Pat Nanton gained honours as the first black Antiguan sporting champion during the 1930s.

Cricket is played informally all year round on both Antigua and Barbuda, the official season running from January to July, when domestic leagues flourish, inter-island competitions are fought and the West Indies team hosts international rivals.

While Antiguans and Barbudans may argue over politics, debates about cricket regularly tip the scales of emotion. The **Antigua Recreation Ground** in St John's melts to a bubbling cauldron of heated joy and stewed frustrations, especially during international matches.

When the test match circus comes to town, St John's goes crazy. The town is packed with cricket hordes on tour, celebrating each island's play as if it were the last. More action occurs off the pitch than on. Souvenir stalls, horn ensembles, drummers and food vendors cake the terraces, while DJ Chickie's wall of speakers at the Double Decker stand deafens the crowds until well after the last day's ball is bowled. Gravy, the cross-dressing cheerleader, is a regular fixture, accompanied by the wandering army of Red Stripe beer sellers.

Sailing and criket
Cricket and sailing are the mainstay of the sporting calendar, providing occasions to party throughout the year. Jolly Harbour hosts its own regatta every September. The Antigua Yacht Club (tel: 460 1799) holds races weekly, with frequent chances to crew.

The Shell Shield and Red Stripe Cup keep cricket fans in the stands throughout the season. If you are interested in seeing a Test Match, some hotels offer package deals including accommodation, flights and tickets. Contact the Antigua Tourist Office in London on 020 7486 7073 or visit their websites: www.antigua-barbuda.com; www.antigua-barbuda.org.

ANTIGUA SAILING WEEK

With fewer stirrings of fervent belief than cricket, but just as loud, frenetic and ribald, the Antigua Sailing Week held at the end April and during the first week of May attracts over 250 boats and 5,000 crew members from all corners of the globe. Centred on Falmouth, the week combines serious racing with outrageous parties, nominally led by 'bishops' and their wayward officers. Wet T-shirts, greasy poles and hedonism 'lively up' the waters of the fifth largest sailing regatta in the world, provoking scenes perhaps not dissimilar to Nelson's time at the dockyard 'when warships anchored, and immorality of the worst description was perpetrated'. As preparation during the week before this extravaganza, drinks are chilled

Wind in the sails

for the Antigua Classic Yacht Regatta. Historic yachts gather to race, while a heritage festival onshore keeps landlubbers amused.

OTHER SPORTING PASSIONS

The enthusiasm which many Antiguans and Barbudans show for horse racing comes a close second only to matters of cricket. Cassada Gardens racecourse is located near the airport, with meetings advertised on television and in the local press.

Gambling compulsions can be appeased at the island's flashy array of casinos and arcades, which are always flowing with locals and tourists.

Restricted largely to resident specialists, the game of warri has clear links with almost identical board games in West Africa. It is played in bars, on verandas or on street corners, using a wooden board as the base on which players aim to capture each other's counters.

Literature

Antigua's best-known writer is also the most controversial, with one of her most popular books unavailable for sale on the island. *A Small Place* (1988) by US-based Jamaica Kincaid vilified the country's government and challenged the way things were done, or more specifically not done, on the island. The society as a whole was portrayed as a rusting relic of imperial days, the former colonial masters having been replaced by devious politicians. The war of words against the administration is entertainingly continued on a more regular basis by the weekly *Outlet* and the *Daily Observer* newspapers.

An earlier generation produced Antigua's celebrated poet, Donald McDonald. Among his war poems, he wrote *A Citizen of – the World*, a utopian glance towards a clearer future: 'One that makes life a very happy living/And leaves behind a memory dear that lives.'

Colonial memoirs have provided a wealth of first-hand material about the islands' past. Mrs Lanaghan's *Antigua and the Antiguans* (1844)

Below: yachting is a passion
Bottom: concentrating on a game of warri

details a fascinating account of events leading up to the end of slavery and the subsequent years. Similarly, Mrs Riddell, a well-travelled friend of poet Robbie Burns, writes of her visit to the isles in 1792.

In more recent times, Keithlyn B. Smith and Fernando C. Smith have helped to compile an insightful view of life among the poorer classes in *To Shoot Hard Labour: the life and times of Samuel Smith, an Antiguan workingman 1877–1982*. For an excellent contemporary account, Brian Dyde's *A History of Antigua* (2000) holds the final word on events to date.

Redonda's claim to literary fame, by assumed lineage rather than homespun wordsmithery, lies in the distinguished portfolio of honorary literati nobility. J.B. Priestley, Dylan Thomas and Rebecca West are among those granted titles to the uninhabited rock outcrop.

Arts and Crafts

Antigua has no national gallery but, visitors' will have many opportunities to view the latest works, in a variety of accessible places. Leading artists such as Cadman Mathias, Bob Williamson, Gilly Gobinet and Lydia Llewellyn display and sell their works in shops and galleries across the island. Island Arts, Harmony Hall and the Museum of Antigua and Barbuda consistently have significant works for view and for sale. Intuitive or landscape scenes form the bulk of the painters' output, while the pottery of Nancy Nicholson and Sarah Fuller captures vivid sea blues and original styles of glazing and pattern. Nick Maley, well known for his Hollywood special effects make-up and painting skills, has joined the growing ranks of Antiguan resident artists.

Indigenous art

Receiving less individual fame but collectively acclaimed, craft workers produce original basketry, wickerwork, hats and textiles at the **Industrial Workshop for the Blind** on All Saint's Road in St John's (tel: 462 0663). The school celebrated its 50th anniversary in 2002, combining skilled artistry with community fund raising.

Festivals and music

No trip to Antigua or Barbuda would be complete without calypso or soca at a party, a club or the Carnival. Music and festivals go hand in hand, but weekly parties are advertised all over the island. Look out for fliers, newspaper, radio or television announcements promoting 'bashments' (dances) for dancehall, reggae or the ubiquitous retro nights at bars and clubs. Visiting DJs from Jamaica or Trinidad are flown in for guest nights, their imminent performance boomed around the neighbourhood from sound-systemed Suzuki's.

Below: Carnival dancer
Bottom: colourful maracas

The significant number of Dominicans working on the island make their presence heard as merengue and bachata batter the air waves of several nightclubs and bars in St John's, with impromptu weekend parties at nearby Fort James beach, when the sandy car park is transformed into an all-day dance venue, social club and bar. Most hotels and beach clubs regularly hold ticketed beach parties, offering music, food, drink and late-night seaside revelry. Fort James and Shirley Heights are regular venues for lively gatherings outside the hotel-organised events. The Shirley Heights Sunday afternoon and evening barbecues, when reggae and steel bands entertain the crowds, are an unmissable event.

Sports or beach events crop up at all seasons, offering a rich array of 'bashment' opportunities.

As an alternative to dancehall or reggae, the Antiguan jazz festival in October has gained an international reputation and attracts a dedicated following, while every Sunday, rousing gospel music can be savoured at the plethora of churches and chapels. Sundays are still very much a day of rest. St John's closes down, people dress in their formal Sunday best, and the only competition to choral highs is the latest trend of 'sawn-off' car exhausts, modified to maximise the growl of Toyota Corollas as they grunt up St Mary's Street.

CARNIVAL

Nothing matches Carnival in terms of charisma, entertainment and energy levels. For ten days running up to the first Tuesday in August, music and festivities erupt over all parts of St John's, with smaller scale sprees scattered across the island to coincide with the festivities. Not to be outdone, Barbuda organises the Caribara Festival in June, attracting many performers and party-goers across the waters from Antigua and beyond.

Before the end of slavery, Christmas was the busiest festive time of the year, when planters mimicked John Bull or posed as kilted High-landers at great balls, while the slaves were allowed time to gather and pool resources for their own entertainment. Lang Ghostwas, a towering

Hot air
In January, the hot-air balloon festival fills the blue skies with a brightly coloured barrage of bubbles, a unique sight in the Caribbean.

Steel drums at rest

mannequin, paraded the capital's streets causing mischief. Today, stilted Moko Jumbies follow suit, but crucially the carnival has moved to the start of August, marking the day of emancipation in 1834 for Antigua's enslaved labourers.

CALYPSO, SOCA AND THE J'OUVERT

Calypsonians release their latest carnival tunes weeks in advance, seeking to rule the radio waves and be crowned King or Queen of Calypso. Local musical nobility includes King Short Shirt, King Obstinate, The Mighty Swallow, Chalice and Onyan. Even before new tunes are pre-launched on an expectant public, carnival parade crews have begun glueing and stitching together a bevy of brilliant and bizarre costumes. These 'Mas Camps' commandeer dilapidated downtown headquarters for the carnival preparations, holding parties en route before the final presentation of the latest look. Silk Dus on St Mary's Street and Dynamics on Long Street have recently held open house where interested visitors can stop by, look at what's going on and help if they want to.

Dancer at Shirley Heights

Calypso and soca have been fused from Trinidadian sounds, while reggae, dancehall and steel bands add to the musical ensemble, drumming up the crowds at Carnival City, usually known as the Recreation Ground in St John's. An adjacent festival village operates as a refuelling stop for the traffic of hungry and thirsty party folk.

Burning Flames, a celebrated soca group, have consistently opened the festival with musical sparring in the 'Lion's Den'. Steel bands beat it out to win the coveted Panorama prize for the best sounds. More than a week's worth of beauty pageants and competitive calypso eventually culminate in *J'ouvert*, the 'jump-up' finale with non-stop dancing and music from Monday evening to Tuesday dawn. As daybreak throws light on the embers of bacchanal, survivors share breakfast and sore heads or feet. The final day leads with floats and a costume parade, mopping up partied-out people before packing away sequins, glad rags and sound systems until the following year.

FOOD AND DRINK

Antigua offers a wide variety of food, from authentic Caribbean and specifically Antiguan dishes, to those with strong European influences. There are places serving shepherds pie and fish and chips; there are a few fine French restaurants and some excellent Italian ones; and the resort hotels all serve 'international' dishes, with distinct local differences.

But trying local food is an enjoyable part of any holiday, and Antigua has a lot of specialities that should not be missed. The food is not excessively spicy, although hot pepper sauce can be found on many restaurant tables. Several varieties of fresh chillis are found in the markets and some are very fiery. Nutmeg is used a lot, and is good grated onto rum-based drinks.

FRUIT AND VEGETABLES

Antigua is one of the driest of the Caribbean islands, which means that some fruit and vegetables have to be imported from Dominica and other islands. But a number of exotic varieties are grown here. Breadfruit, dark green on the outside, with yellowish flesh, is full of vitamins, and mainly used as a vegetable – dull when boiled, good when baked or fried.

Dasheen and eddo are used like potatoes; while callaloo, a leafy spinach-like vegetable, can be a side dish or made into soup. Ducana, which you see on many menus, is delicious. The huge leaves of the coccoloba tree are used to wrap a mixture of spiced and grated sweet potatoes, coconut and flour; when cooked, the leaf is discarded. Pumpkin and okra are widely used, as is sweetcorn, and tomatoes, bursting with flavour.

Beach-side shop and café

A wonderful selection of fruit is available: mango, water melon, guava, papaya (paw paw), passion fruit and, of course, bananas and plantains. The latter look like large bananas, but have to be cooked – fried, boiled or ground into a flour – and are served as a main course side dish. And don't forget coconuts, which grow on the tall palms. On the beach, vendors will split and sell them to you with a straw so that you can drink the milk inside. Many of these fruits are also crushed into juice or used to make ice cream, jams and jellies. The indigenous black pineapple, of course, must not be missed.

FISH AND MEAT

Fish and shellfish are abundant in Antigua, although lobster is usually expensive. Conch (pronounced *konk*) is served in salads or as fritters – great, either way. Red snapper, grouper, swordfish and mahi mahi (dorado), and wahoo, which has a tuna-like taste and texture, are all good.

Chicken and spare ribs are the most commonly eaten meats and both may be served with a spicy Creole sauce.

Special dishes

There are some local dishes that pop up on menus all the time and are well worth trying. One is fungee (also spelled foongee and fungi), a mixture of cornmeal and okra, usually eaten with fish or meat. Salt fish is dried cod, often served with peppers, onions and lime. Pepperpot stew is a tasty mixture of beef or pork with okra and pumpkin and sometimes dumplings. Goat water or curry and bull-foot soup often appear, along with souse – pork cooked with lime, onions, peppers and spices. Rice and beans speaks for itself and can be very good. Pumpkin soup is wholesome and coconut soup worth trying for the novelty.

Restaurant Selection

$$$ Expensive = over US$50; $$ moderate = US$16–50; $ Inexpensive = under US$15.

St John's

Commissioner Grill, Commissioner Alley and Redcliffe Street, tel: 462 1883. In an old tamarind warehouse. Local specialities include good fungee and red snapper. Daily 10am–11pm. $

Chutneys, Fort Road (5-minutes' drive from St John's centre), tel: 462 2977. Authentic Indian dishes, large choice of seafood. Tues–Sun, dinner only. $$

Hemingway's, St Mary's Street, tel: 462 2763. Caribbean food, and a cool verandah overlooking St Mary's Street and Heritage Quay. $$

Home, Gambles Terrace, tel: 461 7651. A bit out of town (take Friars' Hill Road) but worth it. Adventurous Caribbean cuisine, exotic desserts. Elegant but relaxed. Dinner only. $$

The Hub, Long Street and Soul Alley, opposite museum, tel: 462 9442. Walled garden; inexpensive local cuisine in a friendly atmosphere. Breakfast, lunch and dinner. $

Joe Mike's Restaurant, Nevis Street and Corn Alley, tel: 462 1142. In the Hotel Plaza. Caribbean specials. Popular at lunchtime. $

Julian's, Church Street and Corn Alley, tel: 462 4766. Imaginative European and Caribbean fusion food served in an attractive 18th-century house. $$$

Le Bouchen sur le Quai, Heritage Quay, tel: 480 1383. Pavement café with continental flair. Salads, seafood and baguettes. $

Mama Lolly's, Redcliffe Quay, tel: 562 1552. Excellent vegetarian food. $

O'Grady's, Upper Redcliffe Street, tel: 462 5392. Good English pub grub. Popular bar. Lunch and dinner. $

Redcliffe Tavern, Redcliffe Quay, tel: 461 4557. In an old warehouse, the tavern serves great island food, such as conch fritters and jerk chicken with plantain. Mon–Sat, open all day. $$

North Coast

Amigos Mexican Café, Runaway Bay, tel: 562 1542. Authentic Mexican food and a breezy garden by the beach. Closed Tues. $$

Bay House Restaurant, Tradewinds Hotel, tel: 462 1223. Overlooking Dickenson Bay, with fantastic views. Innovative international cuisine. $$

Coconut Grove, Siboney Beach Club, Dickenson Bay, tel: 462 1538. On the beach, this tropical, open-air restaurant specialises in seafood with a European flair. Live entertainment some evenings. Daily, lunch and dinner. $$

Lashings Beach Café and Inn, Runaway Bay, tel:462 4438. Great Tex-Mex food and 24-hour bar with live entertainment. $

Le Bistro, Hodges Bay, tel: 462 3881. Elegant restaurant with a distinctly French menu. Specialities include lobster bisque, rack of lamb, Dover sole. Dinner only; closed Mon and mid-May to end of July. $$$

Millers by the Sea, Fort James Beach, tel: 462 9414. Popular local spot. Seafood specials. Live music. $$

West Coast

Chez Pascal, Galley Bay Hill, tel: 462 3232. Probably the best French food on the island. Daily from 11am. Extensive wine list. Reservations. $$$

Coca's, Valley Road, tel: 462 9700. Attractive wooden house with gingerbread architecture and fabulous view over the beach and Jolly Harbour. Seafood specials. $$

Curtain Bluff, Old Road, tel: 463 8400. First-class food and renowned wine cellar. Casually elegant dress code. Reservations essential. $$$

Steely Bar and Restaurant, Jolly Harbour, tel: 462 6260. Caribbean food. Lively bar. Satellite sports coverage. Breakfast, lunch, dinner. **$**
Turner's Beach Bar, Turner's Beach, tel: 464 9133. Lively spot on a beautiful beach. Home-cooked food. Breakfast, lunch and dinner. **$**

English Harbour area

Abracadabra, just outside Nelson's Dockyard, tel: 460 2701. Italian owned; homemade pasta, fresh seafood, grilled meat. Live jazz and reggae. Reservations advisable. **$$**
Admiral's Inn, Nelson's Dockyard, tel: 460 1027/1153. Eat in the 200-year-old inn or the open courtyard. Local and international dishes. The rum punch is excellent. Daily for breakfast, lunch, dinner. **$$**
Colombo's, Galleon Beach, tel: 460 1452. Huge variety of home-made pasta. Entrées of veal, tournedos Rossini, suckling pig. Daily, lunch and dinner. **$$**
Copper and Lumber Store, Nelson's Dockyard, tel: 460 1058. International food and lots of seafood in the Mainbrace, an English style pub and the more formal Wardroom. Both frequented by the yachting crowd. **$$**
Eden Café, next to Abracadabra, tel: 460 2701. In a 300-year-old building, this Mediterranean-style café with a Caribbean flair has breakfast specials (100 percent fruit smoothies and fresh French pastries), a variety of salads and good sandwiches. Daily 9am–3.30pm, Fri–Sat midnight–4am for sandwiches and coffee for the late night crowd. Closed Sun. Cash only. **$$**
The Inn at English Harbour, tel: 460 1014. Well-prepared international cuisine served on a candlelit terrace. **$$**
The Last Lemming, tel: 460 6910. Under Antigua Yacht Club with panoramic views. A yachty haven. Mon–Sat lunch and dinner, Sun famous brunch 10.30am–3pm. **$$**
Mad Mongoose, tel: 465 7900. Lively and usually packed. Simple local dishes and snacks. Sun brunch. Closed Mon. **$$**
Shirley Heights Lookout, tel: 460-1785. Spectacular view of Nelson's Dockyard and the harbour. Specialities include lobster, fresh fish and pumpkin soup. Daily 9am–10pm. Barbecue and steel and reggae bands entertain on Sun 3–10pm, as you watch the sunset. **$$**

Lashings Beach Café

Trappas, tel: 562 3534. Small lively bar and casual restaurant. Every dish around $10, every drink $3.50. $

Southeast

Alberto's, Willoughby Bay, tel: 460 3000. A bit out of the way but worth it. Delicious Italian food in an open-air tropical setting. Specialities include conch salad, snapper and linguine with clams. Dinner only; closed Mon. Reservations essential. $$

Beach House Restaurant, Long Bay Hotel, Long Bay, tel: 463 2005. Right on the water's edge on a beautiful beach, this casual open-air restaurant serves sandwiches, salads, burgers, and special island drinks at lunchtime. Customers are provided with beach loungers. $

Harmony Hall, Nonsuch Bay, Near Freetown. tel: 460 4120. One of Antigua's finest restaurants, set in the grounds of an old sugar plantation with the mill converted to an attractive bar. Italian chefs specialise in international and Caribbean seafood dishes. Lunch daily; Fri and Sat lunch and dinner. Closed mid-May to end Oct. $$

Harry's Beach Bar, Half Moon Bay, tel: 460 4402. Local beach bar and restaurant. Antiguan specialities include goat water, conch water, fish water (all varieties of soups and stews and all much nicer than they sound) as well as burgers and sandwiches. $

The Hideout, Mamora Bay, tel: 460 3666. Near St James' Club entrance. Friendly atmosphere, excellent fish. Dinner only; closed Thur. $$

Barbuda

There are very few restaurants on Barbuda, but you could try:

Jackie's Seafood Bar, Codrington, tel: 460 0408. Fresh seafood. $

Palm Tree Restaurant, Codrington, tel: 460 0517. Fresh-baked bread, lobster and burgers. $

Nightlife

Nightlife in Antigua can mean many things, from beach bars where you can have a drink and enjoy the tropical sunset, to romantic restaurants, glitzy casinos discos or sports bars. If you want local nightlife, you can just hang out in bars and listen to steel bands, reggae or rap. If you're feeling homesick, there are English pubs with darts and pool. Visit www.antiguanice.com or check local papers (see page 119) for special events.

Casinos

Jo Mike's Casino, tel: 462 1142, Nevis and Corn Alley, St John's. Table games, slot machines and progressive jackpot.

Kings Casino, Heritage Quay, tel: 462 1727. Blackjack, slots, roulette, craps, Caribbean stud poker. Also has a sports bar with 10-ft (3-m) TV screens.

Casino Riviera, Runaway Bay, tel: 562 6262. Blackjack, roulette, Caribbean stud poker, progressive jackpot, hot slots. Race and sports book. Live entertainment. Restaurant.

Coral Reef Casino, Jolly Harbour, tel: 462 7775. American roulette, blackjack, Caribbean stud poker, progressive poker, slots machine.

Nightclubs

Outback Night Club, Dickenson Bay at Putters, tel: 560 4653. Mainly attracts a teenage crowd.

Bamboo Strip Sports Bar, Cedar Grove, tel: 460 5199. Happy hours 5.30–7.30pm daily. Casual sports bar with pool tables. Attracts local crowd.

The New 18 Karet Gold Lashings Beach Bar, Runaway Beach, tel: 462 4438. Open 24 hours a day. Live music Fri and Sat. Daily happy hours 11am–noon and 5–7pm. Lively and extremely popular night spot.

Dogwater Tavern, Jolly Harbour, tel: 462 6550. Pool table and lively bar.

Playbach, English Harbour, tel: 460 6575. Popular bar; pool tables and live entertainment.

Many of the restaurants mentioned have lively bars, some with live music. There is live music in all the resort hotels, although it is often bland and geared to middle-of-the-road tastes.

ACTIVE HOLIDAYS

Activity in Antigua generally takes place on the water. Windsurfing is highly popular in the frisky waters off the east coast and among the more sheltered bays of western waters.

Beneath the surf, diving opportunities are spectacular. Fringing barrier reefs, caverns, walls and over 300 wrecks in Barbudan and Antiguan waters provide a wealth of adventure, matched by the abundant aquatic life. Nurse sharks, parrot fish, eels, stingrays and lobsters are common sights along Cades Reef, The Chimney or around wrecks such as the *Andes* and the *Jetias*. Snorkelling opportunities abound in every bay, while further out, chartered deep sea fishing trips will land tuna, wahoo, kingfish and dorado.

There are numerous reputable companies who organise trips and schedules. The following list includes some of the best known.

Adventure Antigua, tel: 727 3261. Eco tours on a power boat, include snorkelling, fishing, reef exploration.
Antigua Paddles Kayak Eco Tour, tel: 463 1944; fax: 463 3344. Sea kayaking and snorkelling; includes a visit to Great Bird Island.
Deep Bay Divers, tel/fax: 463 8000. Dickenson Bay area. Daily trips for certified divers; certification courses also available.
Dive Antigua, tel/fax: 462 3483. Based in Dickenson Bay. Offers NAUI and PADI programmes.
Dockyard Divers, tel: 460 1178; fax: 460 1179. Wide range of options, from introduction to diving and one-day courses to a range of PADI courses.
Excellence, tel: 480 1225/1226. Snorkelling and scuba diving from a luxurious catamaran. The captain is a qualified scuba instructor.

Franco's, tel: 462 6025. Deep sea fishing and snorkelling trips on 'Mr Calypso's' glass-bottomed boat.
Kokomo Cat, tel: 462 7245. Variety of tours on a 60-ft (20-m) catamaran, including snorkelling at Cades Reef and Great Bird Island.
Octopus Divers, tel: 460 6286; fax: 460 8528. Based in English Harbour. Offers a full range of courses, from introductory upwards.
Wadadli Cats, tel: 462 4792; fax: 462 3661. The smart *Spirit of Antigua* makes snorkelling trips to Green Island, Cades Reef and Great Bird Island.

SAILING

Antigua Sailing Week has already been covered in the Culture section *(see page 102)* and the Antigua and Barbuda Department Of Tourism, Antigua House, 15 Thayer Street, London W1M 5LD, tel: 020 7486 7073/4; fax: 020 7486 9970; www.antigua-barbuda.com will provide you with details of a number of organisations that arrange inclusive packages for those who want to join in the fun.

If you want to sail at other times of year, or try something different, such as a flotilla holiday, there are a number of resorts that offer facilities, for example **Sun Sail Club Colonna**, P.O. Box 951, tel: 462 6263; www.sunsail.com; **Long Bay Hotel**, P.O. Box 442, tel: 463 2005; www.longbayhotel.com.

There are several companies in Antigua that organise yacht charters. Some are based around the Dockyard, including **Carib Sailing Charters**, Nelson's Dockyard, English Harbour, tel: 727 0163; rikdries@candw.ag; and **Antigua Yacht Charters**, Nelson's Dockyard, English Harbour, tel: 463 7101; charters@candw.ag.

SAFARI TOURS

If you want to be active on land, a number of operators offer four-wheel-drive tours. Here are a few options:
Bo-Tours, tel: 462 6632. Smart vehicles and multilingual guides take groups of six to the more remote parts of the island.
Estate Safari Jeep Tours, contact Antours, tel: 462 4788. Tours to Fort Barrington, Great Fort George, Betty's Hope and Fig Tree Drive rainforest.
Tropikelly Trails, tel: 461 0383. Off-road tours to Boggy Peak, Body Ponds and Great Fort George.

RIDING

Spring Hill Stables, near Falmouth Harbour, tel: 773 3139 or 460 7877, is the Headquarters of the Antigua Horse Society. It offers lessons and treks. There are rides to Monk's Hill (Great Fort George) and Rendezvous Bay, where you can paddle in the sea with your horse.

HIKING

One of the most interesting hikes on the island, described on page 88, is

Ready for fun on the water

through the Wallings Forest Reserve, off Fig Tree Drive. Hikes with knowledgeable guides, and of varying degrees of difficulty (but none very onerous) can be arranged through the Forestry Unit of the Ministry of Agriculture, in St John's, tel: 462 1007; or through Regal Travel and Tours, tel: 463 7433, who work in conjunction with the unit.

Hiking up Boggy Peak, the island's highest hill, at 1,319ft (402m) is another popular choice. The Historical and Archaeological Society (tel: 462 4930) and the Hash House Harriers, who meet on Friday at O'Grady's Bar on Redcliffe Street in St John's (tel: 461 5392), organise regular walks with good company throughout the island.

GOLF

For those who like to pack a bag of clubs and a ball on their rambles, a number of excellent golf courses can be found around the island, among them are:
Cedar Valley Club, tel: 462 0161; a challenging 18-hole championship course near St John's.
The Harbour Club, Jolly Harbour, tel: 463 8830; an 18-hole course with fully-equipped club house.

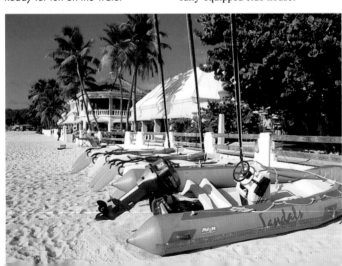

PRACTICAL INFORMATION

Getting There

BY AIR

V.C. Bird International Airport lies approximately 4 miles (7km) northeast of St John's. Major expansion and renovation has been going on at the airport for several years, to include a shopping centre, restaurant, gym and a five-star hotel. The work should be completed by the end of 2003. These developments will much improve the rather sparse existing airport facilities.

Frequent services to Antigua from the UK are provided by Virgin Atlantic, British Airways, BWIA and various charters. From the US, American Airlines fly from New York and Miami, Continental from New York; Air Canada has a regular service from Toronto, Canada.

There is no airport shuttle service but there is no shortage of taxis for independent travellers. The majority of people who arrive on all-inclusive holidays will be met by a taxi or minibus from their hotel.

INTER-ISLAND TRAVEL

The following airlines fly between Antigua and Barbuda, and many of the other Caribbean islands:

Caribbean Star Airlines, tel: 480 2561–5; www.flycaribbeanstar.com
LIAT, tel: 462 5700; www.liatairline.com
Inter-island charters are operated by:
Air St Kitts/Nevis, tel: 465 8571
Carib Aviation, tel: 462 3147
Caribbean Helicopters, tel: 460 5900; fax: 460 5901; www.caribbeanhelicopters.com. Trips to Montserrat, as well as 15- and 30-minute tours over Antigua.

Barbuda and the neighbouring islands can also be reached by ferry or catamaran, on day trips. See the Island Hopping panel for details.

Island Hopping

A day trip to Barbuda or one of the other neighbouring islands – including Guadeloupe, Dominica, St Kitts and Nevis and Montserrat – is well worth making while you are in Antigua, and there are a number of options. If you want to fly, you can contact one of the airlines mentioned in Inter-Island Travel. You can also arrange flights or catamaran trips through a tour operator or travel agent, many of whom have representatives at the major hotels.

Most trips include lunch and a visit to the most interesting sites on the islands (in the case of Barbuda this includes the frigate bird sanctuary on Codrington Lagoon), and most of the catamaran trips pick up guests from the hotel beaches. There is also a ferry to Barbuda that leaves from Heritage Quay daily at 6.30am, returning at 5.30pm. You should be aware that a US$20 departure tax is payable in cash and is not usually included in the excursion prices quoted by local travel agents.

Reputable travel agents who arrange island trips include:

D&J Forwarders, PO Box 2548, St John's, tel: 773 9766/728 0773. Day-trip flights to Barbuda, Montserrat, Dominica and St Kitts.

Bryson's Travel Agency, Long and Thames Streets, tel: 480 1230; fax: 462 5324.

Carib-World Travel Cruise Specialists, Woods Centre, tel: 480 2999; fax: 480 2985; Redcliffe Street branch, tel: 480 2990.

Global Travel & Tours, High Street, St John's, tel/fax: 480 1001.

Jenny's Tours, PO Box W471, St John's, tel/fax: 461 9361; takes visitors by high-speed ferry to Montserrat, to visit all the areas that are safe and permissible in the wake of the devastating volcanic eruption in 1995.

Novellas Travel & Tours, Yacht Club Marina Building, Nelson's Dockyard, tel: 460 1209; fax: 462 3352.

BY SEA
Most cruise ships dock at Heritage Quay and visitors typically have a day in port. Small boats and private yachts can anchor in English and Falmouth harbours and St James' Club marina, in the southeast of the island.

Getting Around
BY BUS
The West Bus Station on Market Street, opposite the food market, and the East Bus Station on Independence Avenue are both easy to find. There is no set timetable – buses leave when they are full. There are frequent departures during the week, fewer at weekends. Route destinations are displayed but it is best to confirm with the driver. It is a slow method of transport but a good way to get the feel of island life and is very economical. Exact fares must be paid in EC coins.

BY TAXI
Taxis are recognisable by TX on the licence plate. Hotels will arrange taxis for you and there are always a number of them around major tourist sights. Fares are not metered, but they are set by the government. Confirm the fare in advance and make sure of the currency you are quoted in (US$ or EC$). Hotels and the Antigua Tourist Board can provide a list of taxi fares to the major points on the island. Fares are also posted at the airport.

If you are travelling to a remote area it is best to arrange a return trip. Drivers are given tourist information courses and should be informative about the island. A 10 percent tip is expected.

BY CAR
A temporary Antiguan licence, costing EC$50/US$20, valid for three months, is required. They can be obtained on the spot from rental companies. You must produce your national or international licence.

Hiring a car is the most convenient way to get around, but driving on the island can be a challenge. Roads are bad, with many pot holes and decaying edges and few road markings. Beware, too, of goats that stray into the road. Street lighting is limited, and there are very few signposts. When there's a hurricane, road signs are the first thing to go and the last to be replaced. The government and the tourist office are well aware that this causes problems for visitors and there are plans for improvement.

Some roads (especially to remote beaches) are only accessible by four-wheel-drive vehicles. Hitting a pot hole can cause an instant blow out, so always check for a spare tyre and parts to change a wheel before taking the hire car. Parking is difficult in St. John's and fines are imposed for illegal parking, but there is a car park off Market Street and one at Heritage Quay. Hire cars are denoted by R on the licence plate. Driving is on the left, as in the UK. Seat belts must be worn.

Car Hire Agencies
Among the most reliable agencies are:
Avis, St John's, tel: 462 2840; St James' Club, tel: 460 5000.
Dollar, St John's, tel: 462 0362, Airport, tel: 462 8802; also an outlet at Jolly Beach Resort; e-mail: lcg8@hotmail.com.
Hertz, St John's, tel: 462 4114/ 1048, e-mail: gregoryc@candw.ag.
Lion's, tel: 562 2708; fax: 562 2707.
There are plenty of smaller companies, too, many of them located along the road running beside the airport. Or check in Yellow Pages.

During peak season (December to April) and especially in Antigua Sailing Week (late April–early May) and Carnival (early August) be sure to book well in advance as cars can be hard to obtain.

MOTORBIKES/MOPEDS/BICYCLES

Only experienced drivers should hire motorbike or mopeds in Antigua. Helmets should alway be worn for safety. Rentals are available from Paradise Boat Sales, tel: 460 7125 and JT's Rent-a-Scoot, tel: 774 1905/1989.

Cycling is a good way to explore at a leisurely pace, but remember the tropical heat and the bumpy roads. Always take plenty of water and have adequate sun protection. Bicycles are available from Cycle Krazy, St Mary's Street, St John's, tel: 462 9253 and Bikes Plus, tel: 462 2452.

CATAMARAN TRIPS

One of the most pleasant ways of seeing the island is by taking a catamaran trip. Those that specialise in scuba and snorkelling trips are listed under Active Holidays *(page 113)*. The following have different specialities:

The Excellence, Redcliffe Street, St John's, tel: 480 1225, is a sleek catamaran that will take you on what is described as a 'Circum-NavEco-Adventure' round the island (also makes twice-weekly trips to Barbuda).

Tiami Catamaran Cruises, tel: 462 2064 specialises in indulgent 'special occasion' cruises, with excellent food.

Wadadli Cats, tel: 462 4792; fax: 462 3661 is a long-standing operation. The *Spirit of Antigua* offers a number of options: one includes a tour of Nelson's Dockyard and a trip to Shirley Heights; another goes to Bird Island, and another to Cades Reef.

Facts for the Visitor

ENTRY REQUIREMENTS

Visitors to Antigua and Barbuda must have onward or return airline tickets and a passport valid for at least six months. Visitors are granted a maximum six months' stay. You should also be able to confirm your accommodation on the islands.

Nationals of the UK, EU, USA, Canada, Australia, New Zealand, Japan and the other Caribbean islands do not require a visa. Other visitors should check with their nearest Antigua consulate or Tourism Board before making the trip. A departure tax of US$20 or EC$50 is payable in cash.

Catamaran cruises will pick visitors up from their hotel beaches

TOURIST INFORMATION

In the UK:

Antigua and Barbuda Department Of Tourism, Antigua House, 15 Thayer Street, London W1M 5LD, tel: 020 7486 7073/4; fax: 020 7486 9970; website: www.antigua-barbuda.com.

In the US:

Antigua and Barbuda Department of Tourism, 610 Fifth Avenue, Suite 311, New York, NY 10020, tel: 212 541 4117; fax: 212 757 1607; e-mail: info@antigua-barbuda.org.

Antigua and Barbuda Department of Tourism and Trade, 25 S.E. 2nd Avenue, Suite 300, Miami, FL 33131; tel: 305 381 6762; fax: 305 381 7908; e-mail: cganvear@bellsouth.net.

In Canada:

Antigua and Barbuda Department of Tourism & Trade, 60 St Clair Avenue East, Suite 304, Toronto, Ontario, M4T 1N5, tel: 416 961 3085; fax: 416 961 7218; e-mail: info@antigua-barbuda-ca.com

In Antigua:

Antigua and Barbuda Department of Tourism, corner of Nevis Street and Friendly Alley, PO Box 363, St John's, tel: 462 0029/0480; fax: 462 2483; e-mail: deptourism@candw.ag.

Antigua Hotels and Tourist Association, Island House , PO Box 454, Newgate Street, St. John's, tel: 462 0374 or 463 3703; fax: 462 3702; e-mail: ahta@candw.ag.

CURRENCY AND EXCHANGE

The currency used on both of the islands is the Eastern Caribbean dollar (EC$), one dollar is made up of 100 cents. The exchange rate is tied to the US dollar at approximately US$1 = EC$2.60. The coins (EC$1, 50, 25, 10 and 5 cents), look very much like English coins, with the Queen's head on the front. US dollars are widely accepted in hotels, restaurants and shops, but you will be given change in EC currency. Major credit cards are also accepted in most hotels and restaurants, but always check in advance. Sterling can be exchanged in banks in St John's High Street, and at Woods Shopping Centre, Friar's Hill Road, to the north of St John's. There are ATMs (cash machines) located outside several banks

OPENING TIMES

Banks are usually open Mon–Thur 8am–2pm, Fri 8am–5pm; some also open until noon on Sat. Shops open Mon–Fri 8am–4pm (some close between noon and 1pm), Sat 8am–noon. The Antigua Tourist Office and most government offices open Mon–Thur 8am–4.30pm, Fri 8am–3pm.

> **Shopping and souvenirs**
> Shopping in Antigua can be divided into two distinct categories. One comprises the duty-free goods that can be bought at Heritage Quay in St John's. These incude jewellery, designer clothing, leather goods, Cuban cigars, alcohol and perfume. The other category includes more specifically Antiguan goods that make attractive gifts or souvenirs: batik, pottery and paintings by local artists and wood carvings. These goods can be found in Redcliffe Quay at Harmony Hall in the southeast of the island, and in shops at the large resort hotels.
> It is also fun to take home products such as herb-scented soaps, Carib coffee, guava jam, bottles of seamoss and, of course, Antigua rum.

TIPPING AND TAXES

A 10 percent tip is expected by taxi drivers and in restaurants. The latter may add a 10 percent service charge to the bill, so you don't need to tip on top of that, unless you feel it is deserved. An 8.5 percent government tax is added to all hotel bills (if you are on an all-inclusive holiday this should already have been included).

PUBLIC HOLIDAYS

1 January: New Year's Day
Late March–early April: Good Friday, Easter Monday
First Monday in May: Labour Day
Late May: Whit Monday
1 July: V.C. Bird Day
First Monday and Tuesday in August: Carnival
1 November: Independence Day
25–26 December: Christmas Day and Boxing Day

TELECOMMUNICATIONS

To phone Antigua from the UK, dial 001 then the country/area code which is **268**. For outgoing calls to the UK and the rest of Europe dial 011; for Canada, the USA and other Caribbean islands, dial 1; then add the country code (44 for the UK) and national phone number, omitting the first digit of the area code.

Cable & Wireless phone cards (for local and international calls) can be purchased at hotels and some shops, with signs outside. There are coin and card phone boxes all over the island. As anywhere in the world, calls made from a hotel room will be more expensive than those made from public phones.
Operator: 0
Directory enquiries: 411

Faxes can be sent from the Cable & Wireless office in St Mary's Street, St John's, from Parcel Plus in Redcliffe Quay (which also has Federal Express and internet services) and from all major hotels.

Mobile Phones

Mobile phones are gaining popularity on the island but do not have the wide range of services provided in Europe and the USA. Most UK phones cannot be used in Antigua. Local mobiles can be hired and pre-paid SIM cards purchased from APUA PCS at: Yacht Services Office, Nelson's Dockyard, tel: 562 3147; Aquasports, Jolly Harbour, tel: 480 3095 (both for local calls only) and Long Street, St John's, tel: 727 2782.
Visit www.apuatelcom for more details

Internet

St John's: Internet Café, Upper Church Street; Parcel Plus, Redcliffe Quay. English Harbour: Cyber Café at Antigua Yacht Club.

More internet cafés are opening all the time, and most large hotels have access for their guests, but beware, resort internet rates may not be as attractive as the independent places around town.

POSTAL SERVICES

There are post offices at Long Street/High Street, St John's, Woods Centre, Friar's Hill Road, and English Harbour. Postcards and letters can also be posted from your hotel.

MEDIA
Newspapers

The *Antigua Sun* and the *Observer* are daily publications published in St John's. The *Outlet* is a weekly journal. The *Trinidad Guardian* and the Jamaican *Gleaner* are also widely available. The *New York Times*, *USA Today* and a number of English newspapers are also available, mainly in hotel shops, but are usually a day old by the time they reach the islands.

Radio and Television

There are several radio stations on the island, broadcasting a mixture of news, music and phone-in programmes.
Observer Radio 91.1 FM
Sun Radio FM 100.1 FM
ZDK 110.0 AM
Antigua Broadcasting Service (ABS) 620 AM
BBC 89.9 FM

Caribbean Radio Lighthouse (Baptist – all religious programmes).

There is only one television station, Antigua Broadcasting Service (ABS) which airs many local programmes as well as CNN and other US programmes. Most hotels have satellite dishes with a variety of channels, mainly of North American origin.

ELECTRICITY

The wattage is 220 volts in some places, 110 volts in others. Hotels may provide currency adapters. Visitors from the UK will need plug adapters, as sockets are two-point ones.

TIME

Antigua-Barbuda is on Atlantic Time, which is four hours behind Greenwich Mean Time (GMT) in (British) winter, and five hours behind in summer.

CLOTHING

Casual, cool and comfortable clothes are what you need. However, Antiguans are fairly conservative and may be offended at inappropriate dress. Don't wear bathing costumes or very short shorts when shopping or sightseeing in town, and stick to the recommended 'elegantly casual' dress in hotels and restaurants. Some venues are more formal than others and may ask men to wear a jacket and tie. Winter evenings can be cool and a light wrap is occasionally welcome. For the most part showers are short and there is usually shelter nearby, so rain gear is unnecessary.

HEALTH CARE

There are no particular health problems to be aware of on the islands. No vaccinations are necessary and there are no poisonous snakes. Bottled mineral water is widely available and visitors are often advised not to drink the tap water – but many drinks are full of crushed ice, which seems to do no one any harm.

Apart from minor stomach upsets, sunburn and heatstroke are the two most commonly experienced problems, and most can be avoided by using common sense. The Caribbean sun is very fierce, even when there are clouds in the sky, so be sure to take sensible precautions – wear a hat to protect your head and provide some shade, use a high-factor sunblock, stay out of the sun during the midday hours, and drink plenty of water. Aloe vera, a natural remedy, and other after-sun soothers are sold in pharmacies and hotel shops.

All visitors should take out adequate insurance to cover medical costs (as well as loss or damage to property) before they leave home. Your travel agent will usually organise this for you when you make your booking.

Hospitals and Clinics

There is one state-run hospital in Antigua, the Holberton Hospital on Queen Elizabeth Highway, tel: 462 0251. The standard of care is quite good. The Holberton will be superseded by Mount St John's Medical Centre when it is finished (the completion date expected to be some time in 2003).

There are a number of private clinics and health centres. The Adelin Medical Centre on Fort Road, north of St John's, tel: 462 0866/7 has some of the best facilities and doctors on the island.

Ortho Medical Associates, Woods Centre, Friars' Hill Road, tel: 462 1932 (emergencies, tel: 462 2219) also has a good reputation.

If you should become ill while you are on holiday your hotel will arrange for you to see a doctor. For minor complaints, most of the large hotels have a duty nurse on the premises.

Pharmacies

There are numerous pharmacies on the island of Antigua, including:
Wood Pharmacy, Woods Centre, Friars' Hill Road, tel: 462 9287/8. Large and well stocked. Open Mon–Sat 9am–10pm, Sun 11am–6pm.
Benjies Department Store, Redcliffe Street, St John's, tel: 462 0733. Open usual shopping hours.
Ceco Pharmacy, High Street, St John's, tel: 462 4706. Open daily 8am–midnight (including holidays).

Dentists

There are many dentists on the island, although it can be hard to contact one on public holidays and at weekends. Check the Yellow Pages for further names and addresses, or ask your hotel for recommendations.
Dr Sengupta, Woods Centre, Friars' Hill Road, tel: 462 9312/3; emergencies tel: 464 9738.
Seventh Day Adventist Dental Clinic, Nevis Street, St John's, tel: 462 9393.
Dr Bernard Evan-Wong, Gambles Medical Centre, Friars' Hill Road, tel: 462 3050/9599.
Dr Maxwell Francis, corner of Cross and Newgate Streets, St John's, tel: 462 0058/2777.

EMERGENCY NUMBERS

Police/ambulance: 911
Fire: 462 0044
Air/Sea Rescue: 462 3062
Police Headquarters: 462 0125

CRIME

Antigua and Barbuda are pretty safe places, with little violent crime. There is a certain amount of petty crime, as there is anywhere else in the world, and general precautions should be taken. Never leave valuables in a vehicle, even if it is locked. Don't take valuables to the beach, or leave items unattended. Don't purchase any illegal substances. Don't visit the more remote, isolated beaches by yourself. Don't produce large amounts of cash in public; and be mindful of bags, pockets and cameras in busy places such as markets and at carnival time.

DIPLOMATIC REPRESENTATION

Resident Acting British High Commissioner, 11 Old Parham Road, tel: 462 0008/9; fax: 562 2124.
Resident Adviser European Union, St George's Street, St John's, tel: 462 2970/2670.
There is no US representation; the acting representative is:
US Embassy, Canadian Imperial Bank Building, Broad Street, Bridgetown, Barbados, tel: 463 4950.
Canadian representative:
The Canadian High Commission, P.O. Box 404, Bridgetown, Barbados.

Weddings

Getting married in Antigua is currently very popular with English couples. It's a romantic idea – white beaches, swaying palm trees and glowing sunsets make a wonderful backdrop. And, given the cost of the average wedding, it often works out cheaper. Some UK travel agents arrange holidays in which the main costs of the wedding are included – things such as photos or a steel band are extra. Many hotels – Sandals, Blue Water, Jolly Beach, the Royal Antiguan and others – have their own wedding gazebos where marriages take place, and co-ordinators, who organise the ceremony.

The administrative details are minor. Couples must stay for five days on the island before the ceremony; they pay a single visit to the Ministry of Justice in St Johns, taking their passports and, if previously married, a divorce certificate. Here a licence fee and registration fee must be paid, if this has not been done in advance. And that's it: all they do then is perfect their tans while they await the big day.

ACCOMMODATION

Antigua offers a great diversity of accommodation; there is something for everyone and every budget. From exclusive clubs at one end of the market, to simple inns at the other and, in between, the successful resort hotels with restaurants, watersports and night life on-site, which many people visit on all-inclusive package holidays. The island also has a number of self-catering properties, from luxury villas to economical Caribbean-style houses.

Off-season rates (mid-April to mid-December) are 30 percent to 45 percent lower than those indicated below. Many hotels offer special rates, especially via the internet. A government tax of 8.5 percent is payable, but for all-inclusive package holidays this may already be included in the price you are quoted. Rates are subject to change, so always check in advance.

The price categories quoted below are for a double room in high season (mid-December to mid-April). For most resort hotels an all-inclusive price will be given on request, or by a travel agent.

$$$$ Luxury = above US$400
$$$ Expensive = US$200–400
$$ Moderate = US$80–200
$ Inexpensive = US$40–80

St John's and surroundings

City View, tel: 562 0256; fax: 562 0242; cityview@candw.ag. On the edge of town, this 39-room hotel is convenient for cricket fans and business people. All rooms air conditioned with phone and cable TV; restaurant on site. **$$**

Cortsland Hotel, P.O. Box 403, tel: 462 1395/0705/1029; fax: 462 1699; courtslandhotel@candw.ag. Business hotel on the outskirts of St John's; 42 rooms, cable TV, phone; dining room, two conference centres; pool. **$$**

Island Inn, P.O. Box 1218, McKinnons, tel: 462 4065; fax: 462 4066; islandinn@hotmail.com. Ten-room inn with Caribbean-style decor, located between the town and the north coast. Mini stove and fridge in rooms, private verandahs overlooking pool. Restaurant on site. **$$**

Joe Mike's Hotel, P.O. Box 136, tel: 462 1142/3244; joemikes@candw.ag. A basic, 11-room hotel in the heart of town. Bar, restaurant and casino. **$**

Pigottsville Guest House, P.O. Box 521, Wireless Road, tel: 462 0592; fax: 463 9658. A simple Caribbean guest house; 16 rooms some with private some with shared bathrooms. A shared kitchen is available. Family atmosphere. **$**

Roslyn's Guest House, P.O. Box 161, Upper Gambles, tel: 462 0762. Two basic guest rooms with adjoining bath in private home. Next to Antigua Recreation Ground. Room only but restaurants close by. **$**

North Coast

Airport Hotel, P.O. Box 700, tel: 462 1191/2320; fax: 462 0928. This modest hotel, the nearest to the airport, has 40 rooms, some with some without air conditioning; cable TV, phone. **$**

Amaryllis Hotel, tel: 462 8690; fax: 462 8691; amahotel@candw.ag; website: www.amarlisshotel.com. Simple, family-owned hotel, 10 minutes from airport; 21 rooms with air conditioning and ceiling fan. Phones and cable TV; swimming pool, restaurant and bar. **$$**

Antigua Beachcomber Hotel, P.O. Box 1512, tel: 462 3100/2756; fax: 462 4012; beachcom@candw.ag; website: www.antiguabeachcomber.com. This 28-room hotel near the airport attracts business people. Restaurant, poolside bar; gym on site. Weekend entertainment.

Corporate rates available on request. Three-bedroom house also available for rent. Jumby Bay ferry departs from the Beachcomber jetty. $$

Blue Waters Beach Resort, P.O. Box 256, tel: 462 0290/0292; reservations through MLI: 800 557 6536; fax: 462 0293; www.bluewaters.net. Near Soldier Point. Up-market accommodation on an exclusive beach, 77 rooms, two restaurants, dancing and entertainment nightly during winter season. Top quality restaurant. Facilities include water sports, tennis court, pool, beauty salon. Specialises in weddings. $$$

Jumby Bay Resort, P.O. Box 243, Long Island, tel: 462 6000; reservations toll-free: 800 421 9016 from US; fax: 462 6020; jumbybay@jumbybayresort.com; website: www.jumbybayresort.com. A luxurious hideaway on an off-shore island, featuring all-inclusive accommodation in 50 units, including a 12-unit Mediterranean-style complex, 27 'junior suite'-style cottages and 11 villas. The island also has an array of two- and three-bedroom luxury villas and several spacious private houses for rent. Amenities include two beaches, swimming pool, gym, spa, water sports, tennis, croquet and two restaurants. Plus access to the Hawksbill Turtle breeding reserve. $$$$

Lord Nelson Beach Hotel, tel: 462 3094; lordnelsonhotel@hotmail.com. Family-run hotel on beautiful white sand beach and private bay, with top-class windsurfing school. The 17 beach-front rooms are decorated in colourful Caribbean style. Open air restaurant with dining on the deck. $

Sandpiper Reef Resort, Crosbies Estate, P.O. Box 569, tel: 462 0939; fax: 462 1743; reservations: 888 769 5074; email: sandpiper@candw.ag; website: www.sandpiper-reef.com. Intimate 24-room hotel on a white sand beach. All rooms have phones and cable TV. Dining room and pool. $$

Sun Sail Club Colonna, P.O. Box 951, tel: 462 6263; reservations toll-free 800 327 2276 from US; fax: 462 6430; colonna@candw.ag; www.sunsail.com. With 167 rooms and the second largest swimming pool on the island; also two- and three-bedroom villas. Water-sports is the main focus with a variety of boats and sailing classes, family-oriented scuba diving at Ultramarine Antigua (andrewmoleta@hotmail.com). $$

Tradewinds Hotel, P.O. Box 1390, tel: 462 1223; fax: 462-5007; email: twhotels@candw.ag; www.Eleganthotels.com. With 45 air-conditioned rooms, phones and cable TV, perched on a hilltop with spectacular views. The Bay House Restaurant; swimming pool. Nightly entertainment in season, popular with international airline crews. Corporate rate available. $$

Dickenson Bay

Antigua Village Condominium Beach Resort, P.O. Box 649, tel: 462 2930; fax: 462 0375; antiguavillage@candw.ag; www.antiguavillage.net. Fifty-four rooms (studios, villas and suites) some beachfront. Small grocery store; pool and water sports available. The popular Beach Restaurant is also on the property. $$$

Rex Halcyon Cove, P.O. Box 251, tel: 462 0256; fax: 462 0271; email: rexhalcyon@candw.ag; www.rexcaribbean.com. Has sister hotels on Grenada, St Lucia and Tobago. With garden; 210 beachfront rooms; two restaurants – the romantic Warri Pier Restaurant extends over the sea (dinner only). Pool, four tennis courts. $$$

Sandals Antigua Resort & Spa, P.O. Box 147, tel: 462 0267; reservations toll-free 800-SANDALS from the US; fax: 462 4135; sandals@candw.ag; www.sandals.com. Top class, all-inclusive, couples-only resort (weddings a speciality), with 193 rooms and an island ambience. Lush foliage, and tropical birds in the lobby, waterfall in the dining room. Four restaurants (including Japanese and Italian), five swimming pools, tennis court, scuba diving and full water sports facilities. $$$$

Siboney Beach Club, P.O. Box 222, tel: 462 0806; fax: 462 3356; siboney@candw.ag; www.siboneybeachclub.com. Almost hidden by palms and bougainvillaea, the Siboney has 12 suites in a three-storey building with a pool. There is excellent food in the casual Coconut Grove restaurant. Small and intimate place. Try for the top-floor balcony suites. $$$

Runaway Bay

Lashings Beach Café and Inn, P.O. Box 2456, tel: 462 4438; fax: 462 4491; lashings@candw.ag; website: www.lashings.com. Owned by the former West Indies Cricket Captain, Ritchie Richards and his English partner, this is an easy-going, relaxed place and the beach bar is always hopping. Only 16 rooms, basic but clean. For the really budget minded there is a simple beach hut (with shower and toilet) that sleeps two for a lower rate. A wide selection

of water sports and activities are available on the beach. $

Southeast Coast

Allegro Resort Pineapple Beach Club, P.O. Box 54, tel: 463 2006; reservations toll-free 800 858 2258 from US; fax: 463 2452; website: www.allegroantigua.com. Beach-front property, with 180 rooms, all-inclusive packages; garden view, pool-side and beach-front accommodation. Three restaurants, two bars; water sports facilities, pool, fitness centre, six tennis courts. $$

Harmony Hall, P.O. Box 1558, tel: 460 4142; fax: 460 4406; email: harmony@candw.ag; www.harmonyhall.com. In peaceful setting in the grounds of an old sugar mill. Six spacious rooms with ceiling fans, mini bars and king-size beds. The restaurant is one of Antigua's finest (see Eating Out). Swimming pool and small beach. Complimentary boat shuttles guests to uninhabited Green Island for superb snorkelling and swimming. $$

Long Bay Hotel, P.O. Box 442, tel: 463 2005; toll-free 800 291 2005 from US; fax: 463 2439; email: longbay@candw.ag; www.longbayhotel.com. Nestled high on the hillside, this family-owned and operated hotel has been open since 1966. An intimate place has 20 rooms, five cottages and a villa. The Beach House restaurant sits on a beach of powdery white sand. Sailing, windsurfing, kayaking, snorkelling and other water sports available. $$$

St James' Club, P.O. Box 63, tel: 460 5000; fax: 460 3015; reservations@antigua-resorts.com; www.antigua-resorts.com. This resort is located on 100 acres (40 hectares) at Mamora Bay; 253 rooms and villas; casino, marina, three restaurants, three pools, tennis, all-inclusive watersports. $$$

Treetops, P.O. Box W1924, tel: 460 4423; fax: 460 4424; gilkesm@candw.ag;

www.caribbeanavenue/treetops/index.html. Five minutes drive above beautiful Half Moon Bay, this two-bedroom Caribbean villa on a steep hillside is cooled by the tradewinds and ceiling fans. With kitchen, living room, three verandahs. Birdwatching is a speciality with colourful resident hummingbirds and bananaquits. **$$$**

English and Falmouth Harbour

Admiral's Inn, P.O. Box 713, tel: 460 1027; toll-free 800 621 1270 from US; fax: 460 1534; email: admirals@candw.ag; www.antiguanice.com. Intimate 14-room inn in a historic 200-year-old building in the heart of Nelson's Dockyard. Two rooms with four-poster beds. Good restaurant with tables in a pretty and shady open-air stone courtyard; lively bar inside. Transport provided to Windward or Pigeon beach. **$$**

Catamaran Hotel, P.O. Box 985, tel: 463 1036; catclub@candw.ag; www.catamaran-antigua.com. Small simple and economical 14-room hotel on the edge of Falmouth Harbour next to a boating marina. Casual, value-for-money accommodation with a family atmosphere. **$$**

Copper and Lumber Store Hotel, P.O. Box 184, tel: 460 1058; fax: 460 1529; clhotel@candw.ag; www.antiguanice.com. Historic setting and authentic 18th-century decor in 14 suites in a meticulously reconstructed warehouse. All rooms have modern kitchens. Transport for guests to the nearby beach. The restaurant offers English specialities and some island dishes. **$$$**

Country Inn Cottages, Monk's Hill Road, tel: 460 1469; inn@candw.ag; www.antiguanice.com. Four Caribbean-style cottages in a tropical garden, 10 minutes' walk from Nelson's Dockyard. The inn has a swimming pool. **$$**

Falmouth Hillside Apartments, P.O. Box 713, tel: 460 1027/1094; fax: 460 1534; admirals@candw.ag; www.antiguanice.com. Sixteen hillside apartments with a panoramic view over Falmouth Harbour. **$$**

Galleon Beach Club, P.O. Box 1003, tel: 460 1024; fax: 460 1450; galleonbeach@candw.ag; www.galleonbeach.com. Twenty-seven one- and two-bedroom cottages, individually decorated, with verandahs. A wide range of water sports included in the price. **$$$**

Hale Inn Guest House, tel/fax: 463 7838; hale_inn@candw.ag; www.haleinn.com.

Idyllic accommodation at Pineapple Beach Club

Six rooms and one cottage in waterfront garden with a gazebo and picnic tables. The Zanzibar Restaurant caters for guests only. **$**

Harbour View Apartments, P.O. Box 20, tel: 460 1762; fax: 463 6375; radix@candw.ag; www.antiguaapartments.com. This six-unit, two-bedroom apartment complex overlooks Falmouth Harbour and is home to many visiting yacht crews. Accommodation comprises living room, dining room and full kitchen. A swimming pool on the property. **$$**

The Inn at English Harbour, P.O. Box 187, tel: 460 1014; fax: 460 1603; theinn@candw.ag; www.theinn.ag. Intimate 24-room hotel inside Nelson's Dockyard on a white sand beach. Two tennis courts, pool, bar and restaurant and panoramic view. **$$$**

Ocean Inn, tel: 460 1263; fax: 463 7950; email: reservations@theoceaninn.com; website: www.theoceaninn.com. Promoted as 'Antigua's premier bed and breakfast', this 14-room inn overlooks English Harbour. Tucked away in a pretty garden with a swimming pool; private rooms and a villa with a kitchen. Within 10 minutes' walk of beaches, restaurants, grocery shops and local bars. **$$**

The Sleep Inn, P.O. Box 512, tel: 562 3082. Located just outside the gates of Nelson's Dockyard, 14 simple rooms that are ideal for budget travellers. Private baths and a shared kitchen. Meals prepared on request. Cash only. **$**

West Coast

Cocobay Resort, Valley Church, P.O. Box 431, tel: 562 2400; fax: 562 2424; cocobay@candw.ag; www.cocobayresort.com. Forty-two pastel coloured Caribbean-style cottages, and two two-bedroom plantation houses on the hillside overlooking Valley Church Beach. Private verandahs, tennis courts and a swimming pool. **$$$**

Coco's Antigua, P.O. Box 2024, tel: 460 2626; fax: 462 9423; cocos@candw.ag; www.cocosantigua.com. Twelve one-bedroom Caribbean-style cottages with private balconies, personal hammock and stylishly understated decor, perched on a hillside overlooking Jolly Harbour beach. Peaceful with no TV, radio or phones. Cocos Restaurant in a romantic setting, overlooking the bay. Guest facilities include a swimming pool and bar. Local entertainment twice a week. **$$$**

Curtain Bluff, P.O. Box 288, tel: 462 8400/1/2/3/4/5; reservations from the US: 888 282 9898; fax: 462 8409; curtainbluff@candw.ag; www.curtainbluff.com. One of the island's most expensive and exclusive resorts accepts 146 guests, at most, in 73 rooms and (mostly) suites. Staff known for impeccable service. Most are repeat guests, creating a club-like atmosphere. Water sports facilities and activities include Sunfish sailboats, waterskiing, snorkel and scuba gear; five tennis courts, squash courts and workout room. Lively palm-shaded beach bar. Top class dining room and one of the best-stocked wine cellars in the Caribbean. In season, a different island band (flute, steel, and calypso) plays most nights. Closed mid-May–1 Oct. **$$$$**

Galley Bay, P.O. Box 305, tel: 462 0302; fax: 462 4551; email: reservations@antigua-resorts.com; website: www.eliteislandresorts.com. 'Unassuming elegance' is how Galley Bay describes itself. A 61-room resort on a pristine beach. Fine dining room. Bird sanctuary in mangrove lagoon. **$$$**.

The resort also has three one- and two-bedroom cottages (tel/fax: 462 4603), tastefully decorated with a Caribbean flair, a short walk from the beach, next door to Chez Pascal restaurant. **$$**

Hawksbill Beach Resort, P.O. Box 108 108, tel: 462 0301; fax: 462 1515; hawksbill@candw.ag; www.hawksbill.com. Among the island's top resorts, on an impressive 37-acre (15-hectare) site, with four private, white sand beaches. There are 111 guest rooms, plus a separate house with accommodation for six guests (reserve six months in advance). Water sports, swimming pool and tennis courts. $$$

Jolly Beach Resort, P.O. Box W2009, tel: 462 0061/0068; fax: 562 2117; info@jollybeachresort.com. Highly organised activities schedule. Guests can swim, play tennis or enjoy other sports. The resort has 487 rooms and all-inclusive rates include all meals, drinks and activities. Larger rooms are comfortable, smaller ones a tight fit. Off-season packages are the best bargains on the island. $$$

Jolly Harbour Marina Resort, tel: 462 3085; fax: 462 7772; email: info@jollyharbourantigua.com; www.jollyharbourmarina.com. Hotel and villas. Air conditioning/ceiling fans. Room or villa only, or all-inclusive packages. Choice of several restaurants in the attractive marina complex. Extra charge for golf course and marina moorings. $$

Pelican Isle, Johnson's Point, tel: 462 8385; fax: 462 4361; email: pelican@candw.ag; www.caribvillas.com. Eight two-bedroom villas with kitchens, spacious verandahs, perched on the hillside above pretty Turner's Beach. Several good restaurants are within walking distance. No phones or TV in rooms. $$

Royal Antiguan, P.O. Box 1322, tel: 462 3733; 800 228 2828 toll-free from US; fax 462 3732; royalrose@candw.ag. Modern nine-storey property on Deep Bay offers 282 rooms in the main building, plus 12 poolside cottages. Little island ambience, but lots of big-hotel amenities. Three restaurants and a beach grill, five bars, disco, and slot machine casino. Eight tennis courts. All water sports are included in the price. $$

Barbuda

Coco Point Lodge, tel: 462 3816; fax: 462 5340; reservations through New York office, tel: 212 986 1416; website: www.cocopointlodge.com; This exclusive, all-inclusive hotel has 34 simple but elegant rooms on one of the most beautiful, safe and undeveloped beaches in the world. Lots of water sports including windsurfing, sailing and snorkelling, but no diving. The 12-minute flight from Antigua to a nearby airstrip is included in the price. Closed mid-Apr–Nov. $$$$

Del's Place, tel: 460 0502/0042; email: efurub@hotmail.com. One tastefully decorated studio apartment (sleeps two). About 10 minutes by bike from Codrington (bikes provided) and 15 minutes to nearest beach. $

The Island Chalet, tel: 773 0066 or 460 0065. In the heart of Codrington. The property has four double rooms, shared kitchen and living room facilities. Car hire and tours can be arranged on request. $

K-Club, tel: 460 0300; fax: 460 0305; kclub@candw.ag; www.lhw.com. Owned by Italian fashion designer, Kriziak, 36 rooms, and 9 suites front a beautiful beach. Water sports, 9-hole golf course. Open mid-Nov–end Aug; no children under 12. The flight from Antigua costs extra. $$$$

Palmetto Beach Hotel, tel: 460 0442 or 464 1585; fax: 460 0440; email: palmetto@candw.ag; www.palmettohotel.com. Situated on Barbuda's famous pink sand beach this Italian-run hotel offers guest the choice of 22 suites and one executive villa. Tennis, pool, volleyball, library, bicycles and scuba diving. Closed Sep–Nov. $$$$

Telly's Guest House, tel: 460 0021/0470 or 773 1943. Private house in Codrington, which sleeps six. Three double bedrooms with ceiling fans. Kitchen facilities available for guests upon request. $

INDEX